Upgrade
your brain

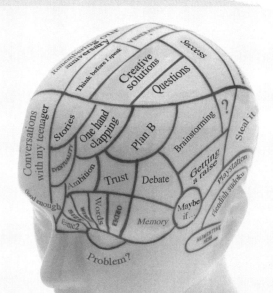

Upgrade
your brain

52 brilliant ideas for everyday genius

John Middleton

brilliantideas

Compatibility warning
Your brain is an admirable piece of kit and doubtless it does a fine job in keeping you fit and functioning.
The ideas contained in this book are equally worthwhile, representing as they do some of the very latest thinking about improving our mental skills. However, there may be compatibility issues when your excellent brain and our excellent ideas meet up. It doesn,t mean that you're stupid; it doesn't mean that we don't know what we're talking about. Upgrade your brain is intended to inform, entertain and provoke the thinking of the reader. However, we don't know your personal circumstances and so we are not suggesting any specific course of action for any individual to follow. It's your brain, it's your life and so it makes sense for you to weigh up carefully what action you might choose to take as a result of reading this book.
In other words, don't blame us if you try something and it all goes terribly wrong.

Copyright © The Infinite Ideas Company Limited, 2006

The right of John Middleton to be identified as the author of this book has been asserted in accordance with the Copyright, Designs and Patents Act 1988.

First published in 2006 by
The Infinite Ideas Company Limited
36 St Giles
Oxford
OX1 3LD
United Kingdom
www.infideas.com

Reprinted 2007

A CIP catalogue record for this book is available from the British Library.

ISBN 978-1-904902-56-0

Brand and product names are trademarks or registered trademarks of their respective owners.

Designed and typeset by Baseline Arts Ltd, Oxford
Printed by TJ International, Cornwall

Brilliant ideas

Brilliant features

Each chapter of this book is designed to provide you with an inspirational idea that you can read quickly and put into practice straight away.

Throughout you'll find four features that will help you get right to the heart of the idea:

- *Here's an idea for you* Take it on board and give it a go – right here, right now. Get an idea of how well you're doing so far.

- *Try another idea* If this idea looks like a life-changer then there's no time to lose. *Try another idea* will point you straight to a related tip to enhance and expand on the first.

- *Defining idea* Words of wisdom from masters and mistresses of the art, plus some interesting hangers-on.

- *How did it go?* If at first you do succeed, try to hide your amazement. If, on the other hand, you don't, then this is where you'll find a Q and A that highlights common problems and how to get over them.

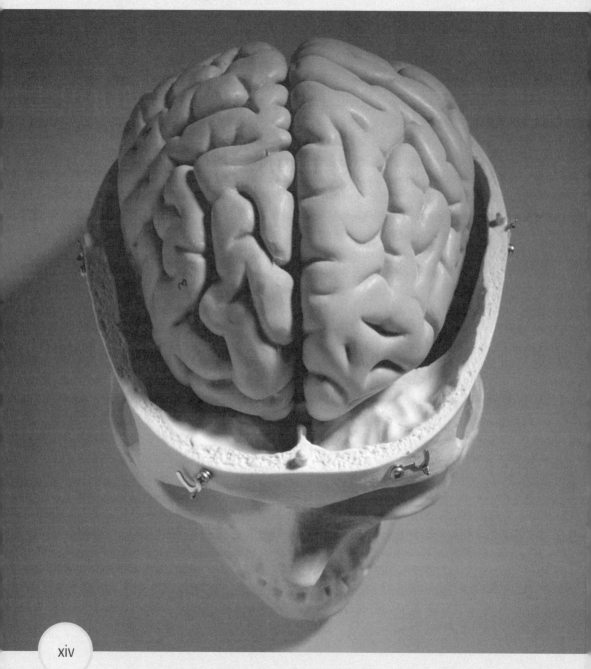

Introduction

It's well known that the most complex object known to humanity is the human brain. (Coming in a close second are the instructions for building a set of bookshelves from IKEA.)

We've all got one (a brain that is, not a set of bookshelves – although that may possibly be true also), and it works away day and night on our behalf.

So what do we know about our brains?

Well, the average brain has around 100,000 million brain cells, and a similar number of neurons. In fact, there are 15 times more brain cells in your head than there are people on the planet.

It's home to our mind and personality, our memories and dreams; it regulates our body temperature, blood pressure, heart rate and breathing; it manages our physical movement, like running and walking; it enables us to communicate, reason and experience emotions. All this from a grey lump that is approximately 75 per cent water, weighs 1.4 kg (incidentally, for fans of the vaguely macabre, your skin weighs twice as much as your brain), and is the size of a small cauliflower.

Although the brain may weigh no more than something that's often going cheap at our local fruit and veg stall, in other ways it is a very impressive piece of kit.

Well, I say it's impressive, but in truth that all depends on how it's used. On the one hand, there have been the likes of Leonardo da Vinci, Albert Einstein and Nelson Mandela, who all used their brains to change the world for the better; at the other end of the spectrum you have those who function at well below their mental potential, for example somebody like…(the Infinite Ideas legal team shuffle around uneasily at this point)…Homer Simpson (legal team resume their billiards tournament).

So how well are you using yours?

Upgrade your Brain is aimed at people – perhaps like you – who are interested in making the most of their mental powers, people who suspect that they may have been running their brains on autopilot, and who now want to squeeze a little more juice out of the human body's most underused organ (no letters of complaint please from lifelong celibates).

Defining idea...

'*Human beings, who are almost unique in having the ability to learn from the experience of others, are also remarkable for their apparent disinclination to do so.*'
DOUGLAS ADAMS

Perhaps you are looking to achieve improved performance and enhanced career prospects in the work you do; maybe you're absolutely committed to self-improvement and personal development as valuable and worthwhile in their own right; or possibly you're just interested in adding to your general knowledge.

Whatever your motives for picking up the book, you should find much to stimulate and surprise you within these pages. Herein lie the harvested fruits of many years of research and personal experience along with insights from the best brains of all time.

And what will you find within the pages of this book? Well, you'll discover a series of prods and prompters which focus on techniques and methods for learning to think more effectively as well as for improving your memory. Many of the ideas for upping your mental potential featured here are highly practical and you could have them up and running in a matter of minutes. Some it might take a little longer to get the hang of.

A number of the Ideas are more conceptual, following the principle that there is nothing as practical as a good theory; these Ideas are aimed at getting you to reflect on (and occasionally question) your current thinking and beliefs about a range of brain-related topics.

By the way, when you get going with this book, don't feel that you are expected to start at Idea 1 and work your way assiduously through to Idea 52. There is no linear argument being offered in this book, so please feel free to dip in and out of the Ideas in any sequence you like. And if you want to creatively adapt any of the content of this book to better fit your personal circumstances, feel free to do so. Imitation may be the sincerest form of flattery, but it's what works for you that really counts.

OK, that's probably enough preamble. The more action-oriented amongst you are doubtless itching to get cracking. So, let the upgrade begin.

Defining idea...

'*The illiterate of the 21st century will not be those who cannot read and write, but those who cannot learn, unlearn, and relearn.*'
ALVIN TOFFLER, American writer and futurist

1

I've got a bit of a problem

Sometimes the problem with problems is that we just don't know where to begin. It turns out that the big challenge is to define what the problem really is.

Let's imagine for a moment that we work in a smallish office and it's awash with corporate clutter — desks, chairs, computers, printers, filing cabinets, in-trays, coat-racks and the like.

To put it bluntly, it's a terrible working environment. We can barely move around the place without dislodging piles of papers or knocking over somebody's coffee. Tracking down anything is a nightmare.

Finally, somebody snaps (not literally – that would be horrible, and would almost certainly prompt a visit from Health and Safety) and they decide to bring the subject up at a team meeting. The problem, they say, is that we don't have the space we need to be more efficient. Everybody agrees that more room is needed and the office manager promises to see what can be done.

Predictably, there's no money in the budget to fund a move to larger premises and so nothing changes.

Here's an idea for you...

How do you know when you have got to the nub of the problem? Well, for years, the Japanese have used a problem-solving technique called the Five Whys. First you come up with a Problem Definition Statement, then ask yourself 'why' that is a problem. Repeating that process up to five times, should strip your problem back to its essence. So if your initial Problem Definition Statement is 'We don't have enough space', you ask 'why' that is problematic. You might conclude that it's because it makes it difficult to keep things ordered and tidy. And why's that a problem? Because you can't locate important files when you're dealing with customers. And why's that a problem? And so on.

But what if events had played out slightly differently? Instead of taking the view that 'we don't have the space we need', what if the person who didn't literally snap had gone to the meeting and said that it was impossible to be efficient working in such cluttered and untidy conditions and asked what could be done about it. Well, says one colleague, why don't we reorganise the furniture a bit? Another chips in with an idea about replacing the two-drawer filing cabinets with four-drawer versions, thus saving on floorspace. Someone else suggests setting up a washing-up roster so that mugs and plates don't hang around on people's desks for so long. Somebody even comes up with a radical suggestion that people could work from home sometimes.

A taskforce is set up to push these changes through and within a matter of days productivity and morale has soared.

Slightly fanciful perhaps, but the point is this: faced with exactly the same set of factors, we could define the problem in terms of not having the space or in terms of working in cluttered and untidy conditions. And the way we define the problem has a significant impact on what can be done to solve it – and, indeed, on how effective and long-lasting the implemented solution will turn out to be.

The key to effective problem solving lies in stating the problem in words as clearly and as fundamentally as you possibly can. Some people call this a Problem Definition Statement. It can often help to write it down, particularly if solving the problem could take a while.

Now that you've defined what your problem is, take a short ride to IDEA 2, *Solve it like Sherlock*, for some tips on coming up with a solution.

Try another idea...

Depending on the nature of the problem, it can be useful to define the problem first in terms of a 'current state' – how things are right now – and then a 'desired state' – how we would like things to be in the future.

So the current state might be: 'It takes ages to locate a customer file every time somebody rings us', or 'I can't speak a word of French'. The more precise you can be about the nature of the problem the better, because that means you're more likely to be starting your problem solving in the right place.

'A problem well-defined is half-solved.'
JOHN DEWEY, American educationalist

Defining idea...

Once you're happy that you've captured what the problem really is, you can begin to think about what the solution to the problem would look like.

Some examples of a desired state could be: 'We want to be able to locate customer files within two minutes of receiving a telephone call', or 'I want to learn 500 French expressions, including their word for "entrepreneur", by the end of the month'. Again, it's good to be as precise as you can be. It's also helpful to include a timescale by which you want to achieve your solution.

'The beginning is the most important part of the work.'
PLATO

Defining idea...

3

Armed with definitions of the current and desired states, you now have a better than fighting chance of coming up with a meaningful and implantable solution. So go on then, get to it.

Q **Problem Definition Statement? Sounds like a bit of a palaver to me. Isn't this just a sledgehammer to crack a nut?**

A *I certainly wouldn't recommend coming up with a Problem Definition Statement every time something goes wrong. The problem has to be big enough. If you sit down to have your breakfast and there's no milk in the fridge to put on your cereal, it's not much help going through a long and convoluted thinking process which concludes that the real cause of the problem was the closing down of the corner shop after the new out-of-town superstore opened. All that matters are that you want some semi-skimmed and what you're going to do about it.*

Q **OK, I've got a real problem now. I've been invited to a wedding in a couple of months' time and I need to shed a few pounds if I'm going to fit into my outfit. Any advice?**

A *Well, the good news is that you have a target date to work with. So many of us make a vague New Year's resolution to lose weight but then let the resolve drift away. Find out what you weigh now (current state), decide what your target is (desired state) and then start to figure out what you need to do to hit that target.*

2

Solve it like Sherlock

Sometimes we know immediately what we have to do to tackle a problem. Here's a more structured approach you can adopt when the answer isn't so obvious.

Problems, problems. I don't know about you, but I rarely get through the day without facing more than my fair share of snags, mishaps and quandaries.

Whether it's my children wanting help with their maths homework, a doorknob dropping off or something else entirely, there's always something going on to test my problem-solving mettle. In most cases, the solutions are self-evident – setting up a project team to sort out the knobless door *chez* Middleton would be a solution-generating sledgehammer to crack a problematic nut.

Once in a while, though, a bigger problem looms. On these occasions, it's not always immediately apparent what should be done for the best. Indeed, sometimes it's not absolutely clear what the problem is. That's when I like to reach for the Xerox Problem-Solving Process.

In fairness, there are any number of problem-solving processes out there that you could use. Search on Google and you'll find five-, eight-, even ten-step versions.

Here's an idea for you...

After your brainstorming has generated lots of ideas for tackling your problems, whittle the ideas down to a realistic set of options by thinking about the most important criteria that your chosen solution will need to satisfy. For example, it might be most important to you that your solution saves money, or that it saves time or is accepted by everyone. Once you know your most important criteria, you can really get to grips with identifying and implementing the most appropriate solution.

They all take you through the same essential process but break it up in different ways.

The Xerox approach isn't inherently better than most of the others, but it does provide a structured basis for tackling the decent-sized problems you're like to come across at home and at work. It consists of six steps, namely:

1. Identify and select the problem
2. Analyse the problem
3. Generate potential solutions
4. Select and plan the solution
5. Implement the solution
6. Evaluate the solution

Let's have a quick look at each in turn:

Step 1. Identify and select the problem

What do we want to change? What's going on that makes you think there's a problem? Who is affected? When, where and how is it happening? Why is it happening? What's the point of this? Use the evidence you're gathering as a basis for coming up with a definition of the problem and what the desired outcome is.

Step 2. Analyse the problem

What's currently stopping us from reaching the desired outcome? What seem to be the key causes?

Step 3. Generate potential solutions

What are all the ways in which we could achieve the desired outcome? A brainstorming session (sometimes called a 'thought showers session' in the more politically correct environments) would be the classic tool to use at this point.

If you find yourself short of ideas, check out IDEA 18, *Kick-start your creativity*, for some tips about creative thinking.

Try another idea...

Step 4. Select and plan the solution

Of all the possible solutions, what is the best way to solve this problem? What are the benefits and risks attached to each possible solution? Do we have the necessary resources? Do we have enough time to implement the approach?

Step 5. Implement the solution

Are we following the plan? Is the plan working as expected or does it need tweaking as we go along?

Step 6. Evaluate the solution

How well did it work? Did it turn out as expected? If not, what happened and why? How well will the implemented solution bear up in the future?

'All that is comes from the mind; it is based on the mind. It is fashioned by the mind.'
The Pali Canon

Defining idea...

As mentioned earlier, this is not the only problem-solving process around. There is, for example, another popular model that goes under the name of Fan Dance. It's an acronym describing an eight-step method – For, Against, Now what?, Definition, Alternatives, Narrow down, Check consequences, and Effect.

Whichever process you decide to go with, the benefits are the same. Any structured problem-solving process gives shape to your thinking, offers the key tools you need at every key stage, and – most crucial of all – enables you to focus on the problem at hand.

How did it go?

Q   I've just tried holding a thought shower with my team and it turned out to be more of a thought drizzle. What can I do?

A   *First of all, did you make sure that everyone was clear what they were being asked to do? One way to set up a session like this is to frame it along the lines of 'What are all the ways that we could...?' and then add the outcome you're after, e.g. '...improve relations with our customers?' Once you start the session, it's really important not to pass judgement on any ideas until the session has finished, as you're trying to encourage wild and exaggerated ideas, not censor them.*

Q   OK, I've just run another shower and it went better this time. I've got lots of ideas now, but how can I make sure I sift out the best ones for further investigation?

A   *For a start, cut out all this 'I' stuff. If the team are good enough to come up with the ideas, they're good enough to have some involvement in taking things forward. The key to success here is to develop some firm criteria for assessing the ideas. Maybe cost is the big issue, or perhaps speed of implementation. Once you've worked that out, work through the ideas together.*

3

Capture your thoughts

Ever come with up a great idea only to forget it moments later? Here are a few tips for ensuring that the output of your inner genius doesn't disappear up the mental Swanee.

Ever found yourself wandering around a supermarket desperately trying to remember what on earth it was you that you went in there to buy?

Or perhaps you've strolled purposefully to another room in your home only to end up unsure about your motivation. This one, by the way, is particularly perplexing when you've gone to the bathroom and, what's more, you've locked the door.

Maybe it's just me, but my guess is that we're all occasionally prone to lose track of ideas and odd items of information (not to mention ideas) in these multi-tasking, information-overloaded, nanosecond noughties.

Not that letting the odd flash of inspirational thought get away is just a twenty-first-century phenomenon. Back in 1798, Samuel Taylor Coleridge was staying in a cottage in Somerset and was hard at work on a new epic poem, to be called *Kubla Khan*, that had come to him in his sleep the night before. He was disturbed when

Here's an idea for you... **Try capturing your ideas in a different medium to the one you would normally use. For example, if you wanted to review your career to date, clear an hour in your diary. Then gather together assorted materials that you can use to create a sculpture that describes your career so far. After you have made your sculpture – and feel free to be as creative as you like – reflect on what it's telling you about your career and perhaps your aspirations for the future.**

somebody, later referred to by Coleridge as a 'person from Porlock', paid a call. By the time he left, Coleridge's creative muse had gone AWOL and he only ever managed to capture fifty-five lines of his unrealised masterpiece.

While we can't always legislate against unplanned interruptions, we can do more to capture those fleeting thoughts, insights and ideas before they evaporate.

What, for instance, do you keep by the side of your bed? (Please, if you're not going to take this seriously...) It's a well-observed phenomenon that the resting mind regularly throws up solutions to problems or questions that have been exercising us during the day. And have you ever woken up in the middle of the night with a moment of inspiration, turned over and gone back to sleep, only to find that the thought or idea has irretrievably disappeared when you wake in the morning?

OK. so keeping a notebook and pencil by your bedside is not exactly rocket science, but very few of us do it in my experience (one of my more interesting research projects). The gap between common sense and common practice is as wide as ever.

And what about when you're out and about? Bruce Chatwin, the peerless travel writer, was renowned for regularly buying stocks of Moleskine notebooks from a Parisian stationery shop so that he could take a supply with him everywhere he went. Van Gogh and Matisse used Moleskines for making sketches. I use them myself for capturing thoughts and ideas. Before I disquiet my committed vegetarian readers or get a van full of animal rights activists beating a path to my front door, I should point out that no moles were harmed in the production of these notebooks.

It's not only the big ideas that are worth capturing. Take a stroll to IDEA 16, *Little ideas mean a lot*, for a look at how small can be beautiful.

Try another idea...

Notebooks are not only useful for simply capturing your inspirational stuff; they can also be used in more structured ways. For example, you can create a Networking Log to enable you to keep an accurate record of all the contacts you have made. I know one eBay trader who regularly sells CDs, DVDs and books online; he carries a small notebook around with him that he calls his bible, in which he records details of items that sell for particularly high prices. He then trawls the second-hand/charity shops to see if he can locate copies. Only the other week, he came across a book which he bought for £1 and managed to auction for £115.

Don't feel that you have to restrict yourself to notebooks as a means of capturing your experiences. Use your laptop, your PDA or your technological communication tool *du jour*. In a similar vein, use your mobile to take photos.

'When I try to remember, I always forget.'
A.A. MILNE's Winnie the Pooh

Defining idea...

How did it go?

Q   I have my Moleskine equivalent in hand and have started jotting my thoughts down as they occur. Is that all there is to this?

A   *Pretty much so. The key challenge is to make sure that we capture as many thoughts and ideas as we possibly can. It's crucial to capture thoughts as they occur. It's no use having a notebook at home when we have an inspirational flash on the common. We need it with us at all times. Without a means of noting insights as they occur, the danger is that we have idea leakage. Something occurs to us, we have a flash of inspiration, then the cellphone rings. Five minutes later, we've finished the call and have completely forgotten our idea.*

Q   OK, I've been keeping a notebook with me for a little while and it's filled up. Now what?

A   *The first priority is to get a replacement up and running as quickly as possible. The second priority is to set time aside to review the contents of volume one. There may be ideas or thoughts that you want to act on sooner rather than later. There may be insights that you aren't ready to do anything with just yet. To make sure these don't disappear into the mists of time, you might want to arrange a date in the future when you will rescan the contents of the notebook.*

4

Get to the point

When you're conveying information in writing or at a presentation, front-end load your communications with the key summarising point.

Wouldn't life be so much better if more people applied some discipline to their oral and written communications and got to the point more quickly?

Whether as readers or listeners, we rely on the writer or presenter to structure what they're telling us into a logical and readily graspable format. When that doesn't happen, we are left to our own interpretive devices – our minds – to try and create some kind of order out of the informational chaos.

This lack of clarity can be very effective as a device in a piece of fiction, where part of the pleasure in reading the book comes from our being able eventually to tie these threads together. In the same way, the essence of the vast majority of detective novels is that we don't get to find out that it was the vicar who strangled the postmistress until we near the end of the story.

As communicators, we normally work to a different informational agenda. Conveying our point with clarity and as quickly as possible is all that matters.

Here's an idea for you...

Take a selection of email, letters and reports you've received recently. Read them through and then jot down what you think the core message is in each case. As well as improving your summarising skills, it will help you to focus your thinking on the key messages in your own communications.

To that end, there are two key things we can do to get our message across effectively:

Give the reader the big summarising idea first; then present the supporting arguments/ information

Present the above in crystal-clear plain English

Let's take each in turn.

SUMMARY FIRST; THEN THE DETAILS

Have you ever received an email that bears a passing resemblance to the following?

Hi John,
I've just realised that Helena will need a lift home from her drama lesson on Thursday afternoon. Sally's away at a conference that day so she can't help. So can we cancel Thursday – sorry. I'm also struggling to put together the draft business plan in time for Thursday. I'm hoping to get Mike's input but can't get hold of him until the weekend at the earliest. I will finish writing the business plan on Monday all being well. How are you fixed on Tuesday next week to meet up as an alternative to Thursday.
Hope this makes sense.
Dave

You can just imagine the thoughts going straight and unedited from Dave's head on to the computer screen. As a business communication, it's not disastrous but it's not great. Compare it with this:

Hi John
I can't make Thursday, so can we reschedule our
meeting to next Tuesday? Mike's not around until the
weekend and rescheduling would give me a chance to
get his input on the business plan and then produce a
finished version for our meeting.
Let me know what you think.
Dave

For an insight into the classical art of persuasion, have a look at IDEA 20, *What did the Greeks ever do for us?*

Try another idea...

OK, not a literary prize-winner, but a bit snappier I think you'll agree. The key difference is that the most important part of the message in conveyed in the first sentence, with the supporting information trimmed to the key relevant information.

PRESENT IN CRYSTAL-CLEAR PLAIN ENGLISH

In his 1946 essay *Politics and the English Language*, George Orwell came up with a set of six 'rules' for writing plainly and clearly. They hold up very well as a set of principles for anybody writing in the noughties:

'I love talking about nothing. It is the only thing I know anything about.'
OSCAR WILDE

Defining idea...

1. Never use a metaphor, simile, or other figure of speech which you are used to seeing in print.
2. Never use a long word where a short one will do.
3. If it is possible to cut a word out, always cut it out.
4. Never use the passive where you can use the active.
5. Never use a foreign phrase, a scientific word, or a jargon word if you can think of an everyday English equivalent.
6. Break any of these rules sooner than say anything outright barbarous.

The secret of success when it comes to being concise is quite simple: think before you write. Work out what your message is and then set about conveying it as clearly as possible. Alternatively, stick with the stream of consciousness approach if you prefer, but use what you write as your first draft from which to produce a more concise and coherent final version.

How did it go?

Q   I've been asked to write an article for the company newsletter. Any tips?

A   *Yes. You'll need to adopt a slight variation on the structure we've talked about in this Idea. Journalists have long adhered to the following three-part approach: (1) start the article by telling the reader the conclusion ('After long debate, the G8 group agree a $50bn aid package for Africa'); (2) follow this up with the most important supporting information; and (3) end by giving the background. This style is known as the inverted pyramid and works well in newspapers and magazines because it enables readers to stop at any time and still get the most important parts of the article.*

Q   They've now asked me to produce a version of the article for the company website. Now what do I have to think about?

A   *On the Web, the inverted pyramid becomes even more important since we know from several studies that visitors often read only the top part of an article. Start with a short conclusion so that website visitors can get the gist of the page even if they don't read all of it.*

5

Buddy, can you spare a paradigm?

A few pointers on how to bring our beliefs and assumptions about ourselves and the world we live in to the surface so that we can hold them up to scrutiny.

Mental models are those deeply ingrained assumptions we all hold that influence how we understand the world. The real challenge with them is that often we don't even know they are there!

They are our set of beliefs about 'the way things are', and are derived from our opinions and prejudices, what our peer groups and people whose judgement we trust think, and extrapolations from our upbringing and life experiences. They lie below the surface of our general awareness, and so we don't necessarily realise the impact they have on our behaviour. Nonetheless they govern absolutely how we interpret and respond to the external world.

Here's an idea for you...

Take one of your less positive beliefs about yourself and reflect on how this belief affects your behaviour. Then ask yourself this question: 'If I knew that this belief wasn't true, how would I act and behave?' Then try giving yourself permission to experiment by acting and behaving in that way. Curiously, you may well find that acting 'as if' in this way can really help to dismantle that old negative belief and put something far more constructive (and enjoyable) in its place.

Often our mental models serve a very useful and practical purpose by helping us to make very quick sense of our experiences and interactions. If we're walking down the street and we see a group of football supporters uttering ribald chants with beer cans in hand, we might sensibly cross to the other side of the road to avoid them. We take precautionary evasive action based on our assumption that trouble just might rear its ugly head if we get in the way.

The real danger for us is that our mental models do not always reflect the truth, i.e. the way things really are; often they reflect what we *believe* to be true. And sometimes we get it wrong. For Shakespeare lovers, think Othello, think handkerchief.

So how do we know which of our mental models are still to be valued and which are well past their sell-by date? The starting point is for us to turn the mirror on ourselves, and to bring our own assumptions to the surface.

The value that comes from doing this is that the more aware we are of our mental models, the more we can hold them up to rigorous scrutiny and get to a point where we can see beyond them. In doing so, we give ourselves an opportunity to redefine our mental landscape.

To that end, here's a short exercise. Try and spend the next 30 minutes writing down as many statements as possible that reflect what you believe and how you see the world. You might find it helpful to begin each statement with the phrase 'It's my belief that....'. When you've finished, go through your list and ask yourself critically what is the basis of each belief.

The key to quality thinking is asking quality questions. For some good examples, nip along to IDEA 30, *Questions, questions.*

Try another idea...

Let's say one of your beliefs is that eating carrots helps you see better in the dark. Where does that belief come from? Your parents? An experience you had once? Something a mate told you down the pub? An advertisement by the Carrot Marketing Board?

The truth of the eating-carrots-improves-night-vision belief can, of course, be readily established. Ask your optician, or spend a few moments Googling around the net, and you'll pretty quickly identify it as a myth (as indeed, and perhaps more tragically, is the Carrot Marketing Board).

'Argue for your limitations, and sure enough, they're yours.'
RICHARD BACH, author

Defining idea...

But what about our more subjective beliefs? Many of these are not about the way things truly are but rather how we choose to see the world around us. For example, many of us hold assumptions about the world that are just plain unhelpful to the would-be brain upgrader. I've come across many people who believe that they have little or nothing to learn from anybody younger than them. I've met others who similarly dismiss blondes, sports fans, the Welsh and so on.

'Please don't disillusion me. I haven't had breakfast yet.'
ORSON SCOTT CARD, author

Defining idea...

On the other hand, don't you think that you are far more likely to learn and grow if you choose to believe that you can learn something from everybody you meet, no matter what their age, nationality, hair colour, etc.

Look, this is not just wishy-washy liberal nonsense about the merits of having a more enlightened outlook, it's about giving you and your brain the chance to get more out of your life experiences by challenging the beliefs – often self-limiting – that we currently hold about the way we are and the world is.

But, of course, you don't have to believe me.

How did it go?

Q I'm struggling with this one. Are you saying that mental models are a good thing or a bad thing?

A I'm not sure that's quite the way to frame the question. They can be good and bad simultaneously. They are good in that they help us make rapid sense of the world by providing mental yardsticks against which we can assess our experiences. The danger is that they can limit our thinking also.

Q Can you give an example?

A Alright. If you believe that you don't have the brainpower to pursue and gain a post-graduate qualification, you are unlikely to make any significant effort in that direction. But what if you're wrong and the belief you have about your academic potential is ill-founded? You've closed a door unnecessarily.

6

Watch out for discontinuities

Ever had a feeling in your water that something just isn't quite right and that change is afoot? Chances are that your hunch is spot on.

There is a well-known aphorism — possibly Chinese, possibly Klingon — that if you want to find out about water, don't ask a fish.

Just as water quickly becomes unremarkable to a fish, so we humans have a tendency to take things for granted, never really questioning whether there are alternative and sometime better ways of viewing and dealing with the world.

I can remember my first day working at a life assurance company back in the late eighties. (OK, so that's not the most exciting start to an anecdote you've ever heard, but give me a break.) When the time came, I was taken, as a reasonably senior appointment, to have lunch in 'The Managers' Dining Room' – a waitress-served, silver-cutlery experience which contrasted sharply with 'The Sergeant's Mess', where 'the plebs' would go for their self-service, mass-catering experience. I caused a little consternation amongst my newfound managerial chums by commenting that these eating arrangements were a tad divisive. None of my lunching colleagues (average length of service: 28 years) had the faintest conception of what I was on about.

Here's an idea for you...

If you have worked in the same place for a couple of years or more, track down somebody who has joined your company recently, say within the last three to four weeks, and ask them what they have particularly noticed, or what has struck them as unusual about the way things are done in the company. Chances are they will pick up on some things that you take for granted.

Seeing the world through an outsider's eyes gives us fresh perspectives on the world. You may have experienced something along these lines while abroad on holiday. What you take for granted when at home isn't necessarily the way it is in other countries. Any of us used to shops being open seven days a week can find it a shock to the system to shop abroad. For example, try buying a loaf of bread in many parts of Germany between Saturday lunchtime and Monday morning. And think for a moment about how challenging it is initially to cross a road in a country where people drive on the other side to what we are used to.

What's all this got to do with upgrading your brain? The point is that in this fast-changing world of ours it makes sense to be alert to different ways of acting and thinking. When we're plunged into a new environment, such as when we join a new company or visit a foreign country, it's relatively straightforward to spot the unusual behaviours or practices. It's much more challenging to spot these phenomena when we are living our normal lives and going through our normal routines.

Yet there are any number of examples of how things we took for granted are no longer the case. Think, for example, about how attitudes to smoking have changed over the past twenty years or so, or how we view authority figures these days. Think about how we experience music now compared with ten years ago.

This is not just a conceptual nicety. There can be real value in our being able to detect trends and looming changes before most of the herd notices anything is going on. For one thing, it enables us to be better prepared mentally for their future impact as well as better able to exploit any opportunities they might provide.

For more on mindset and how it affects our thinking, try IDEA 45, *Ain't nothing like the real thing*.

Try another idea...

Often, all we have to detect these changes with initially is our intuition. But we can train ourselves to be alert to a different set of signals. Here are a few sample questions that can help us break out of our mental ruts:

- How do I know this to be true?
- Do things have to be this way?
- Are there alternative approaches?
- What's the shelf-life of this product/idea?
- If I buy this today, will it be of any value in a few years' time?

'The eye sees a great many things, but the average brain records very few of them.'
THOMAS EDISON

Defining idea...

Somebody once said – I can't remember who, to be honest – that the enemy is mindset. It's only by challenging assumptions – both our own and those of others – that we can ensure that we give ourselves a fighting chance of managing our personal and collective futures to best effect.

'Honour your mistakes as hidden intentions.'
Attributed to BRIAN ENO, musician

Defining idea...

How did it go?

Q **I've had a go at noticing discontinuities, but to be honest I'm struggling to see anything. How can you spot when one is happening?**

A   *Often, recognition of a paradigm shift takes place in stages. To begin with, there is a nagging sense that something is not quite right because things don't seem to work the way they used to. Then these anomalies start to become more and more apparent and create a growing dissonance between the way things used to be and the way in which influential commentators say they could or should be. Eventually, a new framework, a new set of beliefs and practices, emerges to become the new norm.*

Q **That's all very well, but can you give me a practical example?**

A   *OK, let's think about online retailing. When Amazon launched back in 1996, few people anticipated the difference it would make to our book- and CD-buying habits. Traditional booksellers ignored the threat – they didn't even think there was one. Over a period of time, the word began to spread that there was this great, new way to buy books – it was cheaper and often faster than ordering from traditional bookshops. Now, of course, Amazon is the biggest single bookseller in town, and most of us buy online without qualms and in preference to ordering from a bookstore. That's a paradigm shift.*

7

Thinks ain't what they used to be

Some tips on how to go about creating an environment in which you and others can think optimally.

Do you remember the final scene in the movie The Italian Job? No, we are not talking the OK-but-not-as-good-as-the-original 2003 remake.

We're talking the original sixties comedy caper classic. In the final scene, a Herrington coach containing Michael Caine, his gang and $4 million of stolen gold is left dangling precariously over a cliff. It's at that perilous moment Caine's character comes up with a line that goes something like: 'Hold on a minute lads, I've got an idea.'

Sometimes a good idea can come to us when we are right up against it. After all, necessity is the mother of invention, as the hoary old piece of folk wisdom has it. In those perilous situations, we are hardly likely to complain that we can't think properly because 'those soft furnishings just don't work'.

Most of the time, though, we don't lead think-or-die lives. In general, our thinking happens in more day-to-day, relatively safe environments. Sometimes we have a

Here's an idea for you...

Once you've decided what your optimal thinking conditions are, try experimenting a bit with some of the parameters. Sometimes what we think of as optimal for us is just what's most familiar. You might well find that the short-term pain of trying something new yields long-term gain when you find new and better ways of doing things.

degree of control over those surroundings, and sometimes we just have to rub along as best we can in somebody else's idea of a good thinking environment.

Given that many of us now work in the knowledge economy and that we are being paid to think rather than to undertake repetitive manual work, it makes sense to ponder upon the ideal conditions that enable us to think to best effect.

In terms of physical environments, there is a touch of horses for courses about this. Different people function well cognitively in different environments. One person I know feels that she thinks best when there are comfortable armchairs to sit in, orange chenille bedspreads on the walls and ambient music burbling gently in the background. A more hard-nosed business acquaintance likes his office to be awash with chrome and steel, big plants, relatively anonymous wall-to-wall carpet and big windows with commanding city-scape views. Someone else again doesn't care for either of these, preferring to work in what she calls a place of decaying Victorian gentility overlooking a park with a lake.

So what's your optimal thinking environment?

You may know the answer to that question straight away or this may be the first time you've ever thought about it. If the latter is the case, then a useful starting point might be to reflect on the environments that have worked best for you in the past. Where have you been at your thinking best? Was it indoors or out? Many people think at their best when they are outdoors, perhaps walking in the county or by the sea, or maybe just sat in a back garden or nearby park.

If you go to IDEA 3, *Capture your thoughts*, you can make sure that your good ideas don't get away.

Try another idea...

Perhaps your best thinking environment doesn't depend on place at all. Maybe time is a more important factor. Is there a particular time of day when you tend to be at your most creative and capable? If so, what do you do to protect that time from unhelpful distractions? You might find that different times of day suit different types of thinking. For example, I've come to realise that my best writing time is very early in the morning, typically between 5 and 7 a.m.

Do you think best in company or on your own? If it's in company, how many people do you like to have around – one trusted person, a small group, the more the merrier?

Do you think better at the last minute, or does that feel like pressure you could happily do without because you prefer to get things sorted well in advance?

'People think better when they can arrive, look around, and notice that the place reflects their value – to the people there and to the event. It is a silent form of appreciation.'
NANCY KLINE

Defining idea...

Do you think best when you have a specific question/problem/issue you want to address or do your best ideas come to you apparently unbidden out of the ether?

Enough questions for now. But they are worth pondering on, I hope you agree. So why not set aside a bit of time to reflect on when and where you are at your mental best? Oh, that was another question – sorry.

How did it go?

Q **I really like the concept of establishing a better thinking environment at my workplace, but I'm not in charge so what can I do?**

A *Actually, you might find you can change more than you imagine, but let's accept the premise for now. A good thinking environment is partly about physical environment but it's just as important to create the right conditions for thinking. Try to lead the way in encouraging contributions from others, really listening to what people have to say, not interrupting people, maybe organising your team meetings around the principle that everybody is given uninterrupted time to say what they think – all of these steps will improve the quality of your thinking and that of the people around you.*

Q **Right, I tried introducing thinking time into our meetings but it was a disaster! A couple of people just droned on and on, and I could see that everybody else was losing patience with them. What should I try next?**

A *It doesn't have to be open-ended. Try telling everybody that they have a maximum time allowance, say five minutes or so, to express their views. As long as they know the time limit in advance, it should still work. You get better quality thinking from people who know they have five minutes without interruption than from people thinking with no time limit but knowing they will be cut off if others start to get bored.*

8

Think big

Sometimes it's necessary to stop focusing on the parts in order to understand the whole. No, not a discarded line from one of the *Matrix* movies but an entreaty to enter the world of big thinking.

We humans have a tendency sometimes to unwittingly insert a big disconnect between our actions and their consequences.

It's as though we imagine that the decisions we make are hermetically sealed, with no implications beyond the decision itself. To put it mildly, we don't always see the big picture.

At the heart of thinking big is a deceptively simple principle that any problem involving people can usefully be examined on a number of levels, rather than simply as an individual phenomenon.

Here's an idea for you... **Next time you come up with an answer to a problem, ask yourself what the consequences of implementing your chosen solution are. Identify all the people who might be affected by the solution if implemented and ask yourself whether you have taken their reactions into account.**

These levels are:

1. Individual
2. Interpersonal
3. Team/family
4. Inter-group
5. Organisational
6. Inter-organisational
7. Societal
8. International
9. Global

To see how these levels might work in practice, let's consider the general débâcle known as the 2000 American presidential race between Bush and Gore. If you remember, the race was so close that it came down to an unseemly legal scuffle about the status and validity of a few thousand votes cast in the state of Florida.

So what was the cause of these voting problems? Well, depending on who you listened to, you could have attributed the problem to one or more of the following:

■ voters who were 'too stupid to vote properly' – to use a label applied by a member of the Republican legal team (i.e. the problems rested at the level of Individual behaviour)

■ lack of agreed standards about how to count votes, for example how to deal with those hanging chads (i.e. an Inter-group problem)

- badly designed voting cards (i.e. an Organisational issue)

- inherent flaws in the whole electoral system (i.e. at the Societal level)

See IDEA 1, *I've got a bit of a problem*, if you want a bit more about how to pin down what precisely the problem is.

Try another idea...

Let's take another example. Imagine that an organisation has taken on a new recruit, who does not satisfactorily complete their induction period. What are some possible explanations for this state of affairs?

Well, perhaps the new recruit just isn't very good, nothing more, nothing less. It's purely a matter of individual competence. What might we do in response to this situation? Possibly give further training to see if the recruit comes good, or possibly we might decide to let the recruit go.

Does sacking the individual solve the problem? Yes, assuming a more capable replacement can be found.

Now just suppose that the individual concerned is actually very capable. Unfortunately for him, he joined a work group who were upset at the treatment meted out to the new recruit's predecessor, who they believe was sacked unfairly by 'management'. Their morale is low and they decide not to cooperate in providing the on-the-job training that the new starter needs.

'Reality is an illusion, albeit a very persistent one.'
ALBERT EINSTEIN

Defining idea...

Does sacking the individual solve the problem in this case? Almost certainly not. His departure simply paves the way for another poor sap to join the company and experience the same lack of help and support.

Why does all this matter? The point is that the level of explanation that we choose determines our view of the causes of an event or problem. It also affects the actions that we take and the solutions that we employ. An inappropriate intervention at the wrong level is liable to make a problem worse and not better.

Here's a suggestion. Any problem can usefully be analysed at ever-higher levels of abstraction. By considering a problem progressively at the level of the individual, group, inter-group and so on, a deeper understanding of its causes can be gained. As a result, the solutions we choose are more likely to work.

If you want to give yourself a fighting chance of getting to the real root of a problem, examine the explanation that you have come up with and ask yourself the following question: Is that all there is, or is there more to this problem than I am currently taking into account?

Q   **I tried to 'big think' a problem but thought it up to a level where I couldn't do anything about it! Isn't this just a recipe for frustration?**

How did it go?

A   *To a degree, yes. There are some problems whose causes are out of our immediate range to influence. If the poor performance of a member of staff is down to the lack of resources allocated by the company to training rather than individual capability, you may not be able to solve the big problem. Nonetheless, just understanding that it's not about an individual changes the way you address the problem. In this case, you might provide more on-the-job coaching to compensate for poor corporate induction processes.*

Q   **That sounds like a bit of a cop-out. Isn't that addressing the symptoms of the problem, not the roots?**

A   *Sometimes we do only deal with symptoms. But just knowing there's a bigger problem changes the approach we take locally. We should remember as well that perhaps we can do more to solve problems that our not totally under our control. When it comes to a problem like global warming, for example, we can consume less energy individually, but we can also lobby governments to take coordinated international action.*

9

It's all news to me

**How to sift fact from opinion when you read a newspaper
(or listen to the radio or watch TV).**

An acquaintance of mine is convinced that,
whatever you happen to believe, if you pop
a few key words into Google you'll find there
are people out who are thinking the same.

When we're online, it's easy to find supporting 'evidence' for anything we care to believe. According to the internet, various rock stars, members of the nobility, and by now geriatric racehorses live on. I daresay that somewhere out there in cyberspace, somebody has solid proof that the mystery shots from the grassy knoll were fired by John Wayne.

The point I'm making here is that, in this era of unmediated material on the web and 24/7 news channels, information and misinformation co-mingle, and we need to make an effort to distinguish between the two.

Here are a few pointers that can help us read between the lines:

Here's an idea for you... Always be on the lookout for suspect research. Broadcasters and publishers love surveys, particularly when they come up with an eye-catching finding. If they don't indicate how many people were surveyed, or when and where they were interviewed, be sceptical at the very least. Note who conducted the research and to what extent the survey information supports their cause or gives them useful publicity.

Watch out for bias

If you read the same newspaper every day, know what you're buying. Most newspapers wear their biases on their sleeves these days so it's relatively easy to spot which end of the political spectrum they're coming from. The real challenge is to sift facts from opinions. When a newspaper reports that 'PM returns from summit disaster', it's a fact that the Prime Minister is back in the country, but it's only an opinion that the summit went badly.

Search out credible sources

Check the bylines to see who's writing the piece. If somebody that you have never heard of describes a movie or a CD in glowing terms, there's still a fighting chance that you might disagree. My CD shelves are stacked with 'if you only buy one album this year, get this one' recommendations that proved wide of the mark for my tastes. So find writers and reviewers whose opinions you can trust and stick with them.

Check for representativeness

Vivid examples are not necessarily representative. TV and radio stations are particularly fond of wheeling out members of the public to quiz them about the morality of fox-hunting, how the trains are running today, and so on. Apart from noting that the 15 minutes of fame that Andy Warhol promised seems to have shrunk to around 15 seconds these days, pay no heed. At best, such interviews have mild entertainment value.

If the headline asks a question, proceed with caution

Most journalists looking for real information will tell you that a question mark at the end of a headline means 'don't bother to read this bit of frothy speculation'. So for 'Have scientists discovered a cure for premature hair loss?', read no.

If you want to further hone your ability to read between the line, you'll find some useful tips in **IDEA 14, *Trust, but verify.***

Try another idea...

Newspapers thrive on bad news

Reading newspapers on a regular basis might lead you to suppose that the world is terminally depressed. Some folk believe that newspapers print bad news because it encourages readers to splash out on the products advertised elsewhere in the paper as a means of cheering themselves up.

Check out rival explanations

Do multiple sources agree? Does evidence exist that challenges the findings? If one newspaper with a well-documented history of criticising the government describes something as a failure or an embarrassment, it could be just politicking. If a normally pro-government publication takes the same view, then there may be something in it.

'It has become professionally legitimate in the United States to accept and utilize ideas without an in-depth grasp of their underlying foundation, and without the commitment necessary to sustain them.'
RICHARD PASCALE, international business consultant and author

Defining idea...

It's only by deploying our critical faculties that we can distinguish between fact and opinion. It's not always easy, although it seems easier to assess somebody's plausibility when watching or listening to them.

Historically, we have been over-respectful of the printed word; we are more likely to accept what's printed as fact, even when it's a pile of nonsense.

If an expert view is quoted, query the qualifications of the person in question. Do their views deserve to be taken seriously? If they are not named but are generically described as 'an industry analyst' or 'a senior adviser', they might not even exist! Many a reporter has been known to dress personal theories and prejudices as expert opinion.

How did it go?

Q I've been trying to read my normal newspaper with a more critical eye but I still find I agree with every word they write! Do I have a problem?

A   Mmm, there's nothing wrong with having a favourite newspaper or magazine, so long as you recognise that they often represent a particular point of view and that other forms of interpretation are possible. The best and most valid opinions you can form are those that are based on considering a range of viewpoints rather than just one. If you rely solely on one source of information, the danger is that that source is doing your thinking for you.

Q But I don't have the time to read three or four papers every day to create my own balanced version of 'what the papers say' on every issue! Aren't you being unrealistic?

A   It's true that we don't have unlimited time and resources, and so getting a balanced perspective on every issue is likely to be beyond us. Perhaps the key point is the need for us to bear in mind that there are other perspectives than our own, and to be a little less dogmatic that we've always got the 'right answer'.

10

Why use your own brain when you can borrow other people's?

Here's a brief introduction to the merits of networking as a route to increased brain power.

I think it was the late comedian Bob Monkhouse who once made the observation that 'if you don't go to other people's funerals, they won't go to yours'.

At one level, the turnout at your funeral represents a straw poll of your networking skills. The good news is that there are more earth-bound benefits to being a good networker.

Networking has been defined as 'all the different ways in which people make, and are helped to make, connections with each other'. It sometimes gets a bad press from those who see networking as replicating the exclusiveness of old boy networks.

Here's an idea for you...

Could you diversify your contacts? Why not set yourself the goal of doubling the number of contacts you have over the next six months? To help you on the way, you could start keeping a Networking Log to enable you to keep an accurate record of all the contacts you have made. Possible headings to include: Name of Contact; Job Title; Organisation; Address; Phone; Email; Date of meeting; Length of meeting; Record of what came out of meeting; Referred by (i.e. who introduced you to this networking contact).

However, at its best, it can enhance your career trajectory and your social connectedness. It can be a source of information and advice, and can significantly improve your ability to tackle problems successfully.

There are four main types of network:

- *Personal*, e.g. friends, relations, neighbours

- *Work*, e.g. past and present bosses, colleagues, clients and suppliers

- *Professionals*, e.g. solicitors, accountants, shop owners, doctors

- *Organisations*, e.g. professional associations, clubs, chamber of commerce

Here are a few tips on how to network to best effect:

Prepare the ground

It takes time and effort to develop your network. You can't live in a house until it's built, and you can't make use of a network until you've put one in place. To quote the title of a book on networking by Harvey Mackay, *Dig Your Well Before You're Thirsty*.

Networks sometimes have short shelf-lives

A good network requires regular attention. Just because you have somebody's business card tucked away in a desk drawer doesn't necessarily mean they're part of your network. The acid test is whether you could just pick up the phone and call them without them taking umbrage. As a general guide, if you haven't had any contact with somebody for at least six months, you shouldn't presume they're part of your network.

Know your goal

Before you start actively using your network, be absolutely clear what you're trying to achieve. If you want to put the word out that you are looking to change jobs, remember that the more focused the message you feed into the network, the better the chance that something will come of it. 'I'm looking for a senior sales role in pharmaceuticals' is far more likely to register with people than 'I'm just ready to move on, just not sure what to do next'.

Hello, can I pick your brains?

Enlist people to your cause – don't put them on the defensive by appearing to exploit your relationship with them. It's far more effective to ask people for their advice and guidance than to ask them outright for a job.

Networking is partly about making contacts and partly about making conversation. For a few tips on the latter, head for the chatroom that is IDEA 41, *Be a first-class conversationalist*.

Try another idea...

'ETH: If Ron doesn't mix with better-class people, how's he going to get on in life? In this world, it's not what you know, it's who you know, isn't it Ron?
RON: Yes Eth, And I don't know either of them.'
The Glums, characters in the 1950s BBC radio series *Take It From Here*

Defining idea...

I can't help you, but I know a person who can
Widen your network by using existing contacts to give you the names of other useful people.

Keep track of your contacts
Remember to keep a record of who you contact. When somebody gives you their business card, jot down on the back of it where and when you met them. Otherwise, you could end up with a pile of cards that represents names but not faces. It's much more effective if you can call someone up and remind them where you first met – unless, of course, it was at Madame Fifi's House of Corrective Spanking, in which case a modicum of discretion might be called for.

By the way, if you're thinking that networking is a career skill, not a life skill, you're wrong. If you want a good turnout at your next party, bring and buy sale or neighbourhood watch meeting, networking skills are highly relevant. If you need a couple of tickets for the next big event, then your network can play a big part in helping you locate them.

Q **I'd like to network more but I only have a handful of useful contacts. What should I do?**

How did it go?

A *You could diversify your contacts. For example, remember those four main types of network: personal, work, professionals, and organisations? If you know just five people in each of those four categories, and those five people can each connect you to five more people, that's a hundred people more already.*

Q **Oh dear, that all sounds very energy sapping. Isn't there a less intensive way to use networking?**

A *Rather than think of networking as a quantity game, focus your energy on identifying and following up your high-value contacts. They could be president or chair of a particular society or group, or somebody who has particular good contacts in a company you would love to work for. But concentrate on people who are themselves very well networked already.*

11

What are the chances of that happening?

If you've ever been amazed to bump into somebody you haven't seen for years, here's a look at why it might not be so amazing after all.

So there you are in the departure lounge, waiting for the call to board your flight. You catch the eye of another passenger who seems to be looking at you quizzically.

No, it can't be. It is. Your old schoolchum Piggy Malone.

Well, says Piggy, what are the chances of this happening? You ask Piggy where he's sitting; it turns out that he's sitting in the same row as you. You both stagger slightly, absolutely overwhelmed and overcome with emotion. It must be fate, Piggy concludes – either that or the pre-flight beta blockers.

Scenarios like this are played out every minute of the day. People meeting somebody else who went the same university as them; people who find out they have the same dentist or hairdresser, or drive the same car or go to the same gym; people who share birthdays with somebody they've just met.

Here's an idea for you...

Really aim to get to grips with the laws of probability. Take a college class. Buy a book on the subject – I'm particularly partial to *Innumeracy* by John Allen Paulos.

Whether we call these events coincidences, synchronicities or fate, the reality is that these occurrences are actually a lot more common than we might imagine.

Take the aeroplane seat coincidence, for example. Let's say that there were 180 seats on the plane, set out in 30 rows of 6. On the face of it, the chances of you personally sitting in row 7 are 6 chances out of 180, which boils down to a 1-in-30 chance. The same goes for Piggy, there's a 1-in-30 chance that he will sit in row 7. So the chances of you both sitting in the same row? When a 1-in-30 chance meets another 1-in-30, some people will conclude that this means there is a 1-in-30 chance altogether of both of you sharing a row. Others will multiply 1/30 by 1/30 and conclude that there is a 1-in-900 chance of it happening.

Actually, this is how it works. Let's say you've already been allocated a place in row 7 and Piggy checks in after you. If seat allocation were entirely random, then he could be allocated any one of the 179 remaining seats. There are five remaining seats in your row, so Piggy's chances of being somewhere in the same row are 5 chances out of 179, or 1 in just under 36.

However, that presumes that check-in staff allocate flight seats on a totally random basis. Let's go beyond the mathematical probabilities and consider a more human-centred factor. What if it's airline policy to try and cluster similar types of passenger together, so that, for example, all the families with young children are grouped together? The fact that you and Piggy went to school together would suggest that you are of a similar age. You are both travelling on your own and carrying briefcases, and so might appear to airline staff to be decently successful business people. So, in reality, there might only be about 12 seats in two rows on

Now that we've covered weasel numbers, you'll find more on detecting weasel words at IDEA 14, *Trust, but verify.*

Try another idea...

the plane that you were both likely to be assigned, and so the chances of you being in the same row are 50:50. All of a sudden, sharing a row with an old schoolmate isn't quite the jaw-dropping coincidence you both thought.

Let's take another example – that old chestnut of the probability of two people in a group sharing a birthday. If we are prepared to accept a 50 per cent probability of two people sharing a birthday, I won't bore you with the math, but please trust me when I tell you that the actual number is twenty-three. That is, half the time that twenty-three randomly selected people gather together, two will share a birthday.

The point is that a basic understanding of the laws of probability, combined with a willingness to think incisively about the true causes of events we might normally consider random, can only enhance our grasp of how the world truly works.

Get other people to quantify things a bit more. When your son or daughter asks if he or she can have a few friends around for the evening, probe for a number; you might imagine two or three people turning up, your beloved offspring might be planning the party of the year!

'*Most people use statistics the way a drunk uses a lamp post. More for support than illumination.*'
MARK TWAIN

Defining idea...

How did it go?

Q **I'm not a mathematician – I've got a life! Is there a way of becoming more numerate without having to carry a pocket calculator around with me?**

A *Just a little unkind to mathematicians, but I'll let it go. I wouldn't suggest that you need to personally double-check every statistic that you come across – that would be overkill. Concentrate on the numbers that have some significance for you and possibly affect the decisions you need to make in your life. As soon as anybody starts to throw a number in your direction as part of their attempt to persuade you to do something – buy their insurance, vote for them, give them a job – probe to see whether the numbers really are valid.*

Q **OK, so I've started to get people to justify their numbers a bit more than I used to. Is there anything else I should be doing?**

A *Unless you already have a decent grip of statistical methods and the laws of probability, think about how you might improve your understanding. Maybe take a college class. Buy a book on the subject, for example* Innumeracy *by John Allen Paulos. Or have a word with a friend or relative who frequently bets – they may well be a repository of wisdom!*

12
Creatively swipe

Most new ideas involve mixing two or more existing elements. Here's how to improve your personal creativity by mixing and matching from other sources.

A few weeks back, I was flicking through the TV channels and chanced upon yet another re-run of the 1984 movie Footloose.

Not a great film, it has to be said, but it was good to see Kevin Bacon, the actor who played the film's lead. Bacon's film career still rumbles on, but these days he is just as well known for inspiring a film buff's trivia game.

The game Six Degrees of Kevin Bacon derives from the idea of Six Degrees of Separation, the theory that anyone on the planet can be connected to any other person on the planet through a chain of acquaintances that has no more than five links. So, for example, if you wanted to connect the Irish painter Francis Bacon to Kevin Bacon, links in the chains could go like this: Francis Bacon was the subject of a 1988 documentary in which he was interviewed by Melvyn Bragg; Bragg appeared in the 1979 movie *The Kids Are Alright*, as did Steve Martin; Martin and Kevin Bacon were both in a film called *Novocaine*, which came out in 2001. Easy peasy, just three steps involved.

If you've got the hang of free-associating, another useful creativity technique is to play The Metaphor Game. It's a way to open up new insights about something, and takes the form: if X (the thing we want to understand better) were a Y, what sort of Y would it be? So, for example, if our relationship were a singer, what sort of singer would it be? After you have come up with a few possibilities, you can start exploring their significance.

The Kevin Bacon game demonstrates what *The Hitchhiker's Guide to the Galaxy* author Douglas Adams called 'the fundamental interconnectedness of all things'. It is possible to forge a meaningful connection between all sorts of seemingly disparate items. Most creative ideas are just that: two or more elements connected in a new and novel fashion. Very rarely, if ever, do ideas emerge totally without ancestry.

This process works in all walks of life. Film buffs may remember that the producers of the movie *Alien* originally pitched the idea to potential backers as '*Jaws* in space'. A British restaurant – The Fat Duck, near London – whose menu has included bacon and egg ice cream, snail porridge, and mousse dipped in liquid nitrogen, was voted the best place in the world to eat in *Restaurant* magazine's 2005 list of best restaurants.

The act of combining things that are not usually put together to produce a surprising outcome is the source of much of the comedy we encounter. Think of all those 'What do you get if you cross....?' jokes that still abound in playgrounds around the world. Often, though, we are not looking for absolutely unfettered creativity, which combines two entirely randomly selected items. Rather, we have a specific problem that we want to address. For example, we may want to raise £1000 for charity. To get the creative juices going about how to raise the cash, we decide to have a go at some free association.

There are numerous ways in which to generate the random word needed to start suggesting associations: we might open a book at random, close our eyes and point at a word; we might go to one of any number of random word-generating internet sites; we might switch on the television and use the first identifiable item we see.

Now you've got the hang of creative swiping, why not brush up your lateral thinking? Go to IDEA 39, *Throwing me a fricking de Bono.*

Try another idea...

In this process, there's no such thing as a bad word. Whatever you come up with has the potential to spark our thinking. In the case of the money-raising goal we have, let's say that we open up a book (...just doing it now..) and we come up with the word (blimey), 'Apollo'.

So now we ask ourselves what the word 'Apollo' brings to mind, and what might those things have to do with our goal of raising money. Associations like 'Greek god', 'moon missions' and 'theatre' might come to mind. That might lead us to the movie *Apollo 13*...which starred Tom Hanks...who did the voice-over for the character Woody in the movie *Toy Story*, etc., etc., etc. This might then lead us to the idea of raising money by getting people to donate old toys, or maybe asking a local cinema to help out with a charity performance of a film.

I wouldn't necessarily say that either of those ideas is irresistible. You might want to keep the process going for longer on the basis that the more options you have, the more likely it is that something will spark a flash of inspiration.

'**Only connect.**'
E.M. FORSTER

Defining idea...

Q I can see the value of all of this conceptually, but does it have a practical use?

A Yes. The process of creative combining can be used to address very practical questions. Let's say you decide to hold a party but you want it to be a bit different. Make a quick note of the main factors you want to think about – they might be something like location, theme and music. Note all the possible themes that interest you – maybe a Western theme, or Vicars and Tarts, or Film Stars, etc. Do the same for the other factors, then try some creative mixing and matching of the elements. You might end up with a Doctors and Nurses party on a riverboat with music provided by a blues band for example.

Q OK, I can see that could work. Are there any other practical uses?

A Lots. I know a family who fix their holidays using the multiple column principle. They gave their columns headings like Country, Type of Location (by the sea, in the mountains, etc.), Preferred Activities, Length of Stay, etc. In fact, it's a useful approach for any decision where you want to come up with a good range of choices. Think about it: three columns, each containing, say, six items, would produce quite a range of permutations.

13

Learn to be an optimist

Believe that there's always a creative solution and you'll find you're right.

Most research suggests that, given responsible and caring parents, we tend to start life as natural optimists. Just watch a one-year-old trying to walk if you don't believe me.

You don't get too many toddlers telling themselves that it's no good, they're never going to get the hang of this walking business and so they'll just stick to crawling for the rest of their lives.

Psychologists reckon that we all tend to be optimists until we reach the age of eight or so. In other words, we have a natural tendency to seek out and expect good outcomes.

However, by the time we reach mid-adolescence, our thinking style and general outlook on the world is either optimistic or pessimistic. Once formed, our disposition tends to stay that way for the rest of our lives, unless we are persuaded or voluntarily decide to change.

Here's an idea for you...

Have a look at some text you have written recently – an email, a letter or whatever. What's your ratio of positive/negative words? Martin Seligman would argue that this is a powerful predictor of future success: by intentionally choosing more optimistic words in the language you use, you can start to become more optimistic in your thinking, which in turn could lead to better results.

Of course, we need to recognise that life events – the death of a parent, partner or child, suffering clinical depression, extended periods of illness, getting divorced and so on – can significantly affect our outlook. But for the vast majority of those who are inclined towards pessimism, it is possible to build a more positive view of oneself and the way the world is. As Abraham Lincoln once put it: most people are about as happy as they make up their minds to be.

You might be thinking that the world needs its fair sprinkling of optimists and pessimists and so *vive la différence*. That may be true, but the fact is that optimists enjoy themselves more, tend to be more successful in their careers, are better at

If you are an optimist who carries an umbrella, it might be prudent to cast an eye over IDEA 47, *Develop a Plan B.*

Try another idea...

coming up with creative solutions to problems, and live longer and healthier lives on average. Certainly, in the context of upgrading your brain, having a positive outlook on life reaps many rewards.

So how can those of us who are naturally less cheery in outlook cultivate a more positive take on life?

In his book *Learned Optimism*, Martin Seligman – a Professor of Psychology at the University of Pennsylvania – offers a way forward. He suggests that when we react to adversity, we are not reacting to an event but to how we feel about that event. Although we can't control everything that happens to us, we do have some control over our emotions. So, when adversity strikes, how we think and what we believe determines how we feel and what we do.

According to Seligman, there are three keys to learning a more optimistic outlook. We need to understand that:

■ every failure is an opportunity to learn
■ we can change
■ success depends on effort

'No pessimist ever discovered the secrets of the stars, or sailed to an uncharted land, or opened a new heaven to the human spirit.'
HELEN KELLER

Defining idea...

We also need to be prepared to challenge any self-defeating pessimistic thoughts by asking ourselves four key questions:

1. *Is it really true that we are helpless in this situation?* What are the real chances of a catastrophe?

2. *Is there another way to explain this event?* Did they sack me because I really am rubbish at my job? Find as many possible reasons as you can.

3. *So what, even if it is partly true? Must it last forever?* Suppose I wasn't that good at my job – I wasn't that happy working there anyway and I'm sure I could work more productively if I moved.

4. *What is the best possible outcome we can hope for in this situation?* Maybe now's the time to retrain to do something else I'd really enjoy.

Defining idea...

'Why don't you knock it off with them negative waves? Why don't you dig how beautiful it is out here?'
ODDBALL in the movie *Kelly's Heroes*

There are, however, downsides to optimism. Like the pessimist, the optimist can have too narrow a view of future outcomes by expecting only positive outcomes. Optimists see the advantages and opportunities but tend to underplay the risks and threats involved in a course of action. This can lead to a tendency to stick with a bad strategy or course of action longer than somebody with a more rational approach.

That said, the positive benefits of an optimistic outlook do seem to outweigh the drawbacks – and of course let's not forget that optimists are better at noticing and grabbing parking spaces.

Q Mmm, as a pessimist by nature I struggle with this 'cheery disposition' stuff. Don't optimists face problems by having their heads in the clouds?

How did it go?

A There is always that danger (not least from low-flying aircraft). Perhaps the best outlook is one that is essentially optimistic, but not to the point of blindness to the fact that things do sometimes go wrong. Maybe the role model we should look to emulate is none other than that pipe-smoking, Beatle-honouring British Prime Minister of yesteryear, Harold Wilson, who once described his philosophy of life in these terms: 'I'm an optimist, but an optimist who carries a raincoat.'

Q I've got to put together a statement of achievements for a job I want to apply for but I'm finding it difficult. Where should I begin?

A We often don't give ourselves credit for the skills and abilities we have, instead taking them for granted. Try writing down thirty or so achievements you have made in your life that you are really proud of. If listing thirty achievements sounds excessive, please persevere. There's a tendency for people to do this exercise on automatic pilot to begin with. By the time you're up to achievement twenty-three, you'll start surprising yourself at all you have done that has slipped from immediate recollection.

14

Trust, but verify

No more need to take lying lying down. A quick guide to getting your weasel word detector fully operational.

Here are Homer Simpson's words of fatherly wisdom to Bart: 'These three little sentences will get you through life: Number 1 — Oh, good idea boss; Number 2 — Cover for me; Number 3 — It was like that when I got here.'

It seems that Homer is not alone in condoning the occasional fib. According to research reported a few years ago in *Time* magazine, the average person is lied to about 200 times a day. Apparently, men lie roughly 20 per cent more than women, but women are much better at it.

Around 41 per cent of our lies are intended to conceal misbehaviour ('It's in the post', 'Sorry darling, but I need to work late tonight'), while another 20 per cent are those little white lies that make social life manageable ('We'd *love* to come to dinner on Saturday night but unfortunately we've got something else on').

Here's an idea for you... **As well as being alert to the linguistic tricks that liars sometime try to play, use your eyes and your intuition to uncover signs of deceit. In particular, look out for: (1) poor eye contact: someone not meeting your eye as they tell you something. Also watch out for people who make unnaturally prolonged eye contact in an effort to convince you of their sincerity; (2) body language: the most obvious sign is blushing, but there are other, more subtle changes in body language, such as hands going up to the throat or face, especially the mouth.**

We are just as happy to stretch the truth in writing as we are doing it face-to-face. For example, it's reckoned that 25 per cent of resumés contain lies. When the CV-verifying company CV Check approaches candidates to tell them it has been engaged by potential employers to check their applications, up to 20 per cent of the original applicants withdraw from the recruitment process.

Against this backdrop of mendacity, it's not surprising that we've become a little jaundiced about human nature. A journalist I know once told me about his ex-boss's motto: never believe anything until it's been officially denied.

Anyway, we face a daily barrage of deception – everything from economy with the truth to mild fibs to outright whoppers. Given that brains, like computers, are susceptible to the GIGO (Garbage In–Garbage Out) principle, what can we do to boost the performance of our on-board lie-detectors? How can we spot a lie when it's heading our way?

Here are just a few pointers to how liars use language to lie:

Doublespeak: George Orwell's book *1984* inspired the concept of doublespeak, i.e. language that is deliberately constructed to disguise or distort its actual meaning.

For example, 'collateral damage' means 'unintended casualties'. And in financial doublespeak, 'credit' is simply another word for 'debt'. When a credit card company increases your credit limit, what it's really saying is that you are considered to be a reliable payer of the extortionate rates of interest they charge.

For more schooling in the art of deception, slither along to IDEA 25, Manoeuvre like Machiavelli.

Try another idea...

Vague terminology: what does it really mean when somebody says that they 'manage a small team'? Assuming we're not talking Snow White and dwarves here, the unvarnished truth could be 'I share one admin assistant with two other people'.

Lack of quantification: 'I introduced a more efficient system for managing overtime and achieved a significant saving for the department' could mean 'We saved £250,000 in a year' or 'Well, thirty quid actually.'

The smokescreen 'we': when individuals use the word 'we' a lot, it might mean that they are committed team players. Equally, it can conceal details of the individual's true contribution. 'We played in the final and we won' could hide the fact that 'I was sent off in the first minute for biting a linesman but the team still managed to win despite me.'

Studies have shown: before accepting study findings hook, line and sinker, check the background details: who funded the study? How many people were interviewed? What was the research question? etc.

'Q: How can you tell when he's lying?
A: When his lips are moving.'
Said of UK Prime Minister Harold Wilson

Defining idea...

Above all, you must learn to trust your own judgement. By all means, take soundings of other people's views, but make up your own mind; don't rely absolutely on anybody else's views. Commit yourself to a personal crusade to weed out the weasel words, and for once, spurn the words of Homer Simpson: 'Marge, it takes two to lie; one to lie and one to listen.'

How did it go?

Q   I'm not sure that my friends will thank me if I become some kind of truth-seeking missile. Don't we need to accept that little white lies perform a useful social purpose?

A   *Absolutely. As with many of the ideas in this book, you can choose when you want to do something and when you don't. Going after the truth is an option, not an obligation.*

Q   I'm getting a bit paranoid. Are you saying that most of what I am being told is a lie?

A   *Not at all. Most people are fundamentally honest and upfront when it matters. I suspect that we have all slightly bent the truth from time to time to hide embarrassment or to put ourselves in a better light. When somebody arrives a few minutes late for a meeting, saying that the traffic was terrible, there's a good chance that they just overslept or underestimated the journey time. There's no value in trying to expose them. But there are other times when it's vital to be confident that we are being told the truth, and those are the occasions when you might want to press people a bit more.*

15

Darwin rules...

A fleet-footed guide to what evolutionary psychology can teach us about the way our brains work.

You might think of yourself as a hip, with-it, urbane surfer of the twenty-first-century Zeitgeist, but it turns out that we all have a bit of Fred or Wilma Flintstone in us.

According to evolutionary psychologists, people today – no matter whether they are captains of industry or burger flippers – pretty much retain the mentality of our Stone Age ancestors. In other words, you can take people out of the Stone Age but you can't take the Stone Age out of people.

Nigel Nicholson, a professor at London Business School, has suggested that we are 'hard-wired' for certain attitudes and behaviours. In his book *Managing the Human Animal*, he gives some examples of the implications of this:

Communication: our Stone Age ancestors needed to exchange information in order to survive the unpredictable conditions of the savannah plain. This led, over the centuries, to the use of informal information exchange and gossip both as a social activity and as a highly practical tool for swapping valuable information when we are

Here's an idea for you... **Remember the movie *Pay it Forward*, which explored the idea of repaying good deeds not with a reciprocal good deed, but with new good deeds done to three new people? It's time to defy your Darwinian roots and look beyond self-interest and self-preservation. Become an arbitrary altruist!**

at work. And so the 'grapevine' performs a function that we humans value at a deeply engrained level. Any leader who takes it upon themselves to stamp out the grapevine or to suppress gossip and general tittle-tattle will create a reaction that could stretch from social and emotional discomfort to outright rebellion.

Team size: our ancestors appear typically to have gone around in groups with no more than 150 members maximum. It seems we are 'hard-wired' to be at our most effective and comfortable in smaller units. Again, there are significant implications for how we organise ourselves socially and at work in the twenty-first century. Create a group that exceeds the 150 member limit by much and group cohesion is likely to suffer.

Hierarchy: when humans cluster together, we have an innate preference for structure and order which leads us to opt for clearly defined social and organisational hierarchies. In this context, both organisational delayering and expressing anti-monarchy sentiments may be going against the Darwinian grain.

Evolutionary psychology also helps to explain why it's not always easy to achieve cooperation between groups. In organisational life, for example, you may well have witnessed or experienced turf wars, in which case you'll know some of the warning signs: marking territory; monopolising resources; withholding or giving false information; intimidation and bullying; and shunning by excluding individuals or groups. All of these tactics can be traced backed to their Darwinian roots. We are by instinct a territorial species, and turf wars have become the organisationally accepted alternative to fisticuffs.

So what do the principles of evolutionary psychology tell us about life in the twenty-first century? Certainly that we value being part of a community and we like contact with others. Traditionally this has been through face-to-face dealings, but increasingly we are using the internet and mobile phones as tools for maintaining relationships. Spending hours on the phone or sending hundreds of text messages aren't just social niceties, they're a Darwinian necessity.

For more on a tradition that's been with us since the dawn of civilisation, see IDEA 37, Become an ace storyteller.

Try another idea...

They also show that we value structure in our lives. We might think of ourselves as freewheeling units of one on our personal rollercoaster through life, but actually we can deal with only so much chaos and lack of pattern in our daily affairs.

'The Dilbert characters seem to know what any evolutionary psychologist would tell you: hierarchy is forever.'
NIGEL NICHOLSON, scholar, media commentator and broadcaster

Defining idea...

Evolutionary psychologists don't advocate that we return to a Stone Age way of life – let's face it, carrying a club and wearing a swimsuit made of mammoth skin is just so last year. Rather, they suggest that we need to try to understand that human nature is not infinitely adaptable and flexible, and that we need to recognise that this will inevitably impact on the way we personally live and work in the twenty-first century and, just as importantly, on what we can and can't reasonably expect from others.

'We may brave human laws, but we cannot resist natural ones.'
JULES VERNE

Defining idea...

How did
it go?

Q **I've started noticing that some of the other departments in the organisation I work for tend to get involved in unproductive turf wars. What can I do about it?**

A   *Spotting the games they are playing is actually a good start. Often you find that telling people that you see what's happening and naming the behaviours goes a long way towards stopping them. Whatever you do, refuse to play the game – it takes two to tango.*

Q **Actually, the problem I'm having is not with a department that's behaving in this way, it's particular individuals. Anything I can do?**

A   *Often it's easier to resolve a problem with an individual. If you talk to them explicitly about what you perceive is going on, it's difficult for them to just wave you away. However, if you can't get them to change their ways, you can either raise the problem with their boss or look to see if you can get what you need from other people in their area.*

16

Little ideas mean a lot

Cultivate everyday ingenuity – don't obsess over having to come up with one big idea. There's value in having lots of little ideas and insights. You'll see a real improvement in your life.

Kaizen is a Japanese term for a management philosophy that focuses on achieving continuous, incremental improvement in all aspects of the work being carried out.

It's taken from Japanese words 'kai', meaning 'continuous', and 'zen', meaning 'improvement' (hmm, no great stretch of the imagination needed there, then).

It's a philosophy that has been at the heart of Japanese working practices since the wide-scale adoption of total quality management methods in the years of reconstruction following the Second World War.

The great thing about *kaizen* is that it recognises the cumulative benefit of a lot of small improvements. This means that workers feel no pressure to come up with highly innovative, head-turning, share-price-doubling ideas or else keep their thoughts to themselves; on the contrary, the spirit of *kaizen* is more likely to be found in the worker who shares their idea for shaving a second or two off the time

Here's an idea for you...

Encourage your family or your work colleagues to share their ideas for making little improvements about the place. One company I know has a Best Little Idea of the Month competition and actively seeks their employees' ideas, and the smaller the better. It's a great success because it makes a virtue of the smallness of the idea and encourages a level of playfulness.

involved in manufacturing a car by slightly repositioning where a particular tool is kept.

What this means for us in our day-to-day lives is that there is real value and benefit in being alert to those opportunities to do things just slightly better. Of course, big ideas should not be sniffed at, but it is equally valuable – and a lot less daunting – to make lots of small improvements by implementing lots of small ideas.

Let's take an example. Say your highly talented daughter wants to start taking singing lessons and it turns out that they will set you back around a thousand to pay for them. If your bank balance is anything like mine (don't imagine that writing books like this is particularly lucrative), then you'll need to think about raising the money somehow. You might just have one of those in-one-bound-you're-free solutions available to you – cash-in a savings plan, sell your beloved Stratocaster or Bernina (that's a guitar or a sewing machine to the non-cognoscenti), beg the cash off of the girl's doting grandparents and so on.

But now just think of the small fortune that many of us fritter away each year and you'll find there are any number of ways of achieving some decent savings. Here are just a few possibilities to whet the appetite:

- Reduce the number of magazines and newspapers you buy.

- Cut out Monday to Thursday drinking: reduce your intake by four bottles of wine a week, costing, say, a fiver each, and that alone could save you the money in a year. (You would also impress your GP at your annual health check-up with the seismic drop in your alcohol consumption.)

Go to IDEA 18, *Kick-start your creativity* for an insight into how to, well, kick-start your creativity.

Try another idea...

■ The early morning latte on the way to work, chocolates, cakes and crisps: cut 'em out and earn the gratitude of your bank manager and your waistline.

■ Reduce your travel costs: consider cycling to work, walk where you can.

■ Spend less on clothes: don't be a catwalk victim – wait for the sales.

'A journey of a thousand miles begins with a single step.'
Chinese proverb

Defining idea...

■ Review your phone contracts: are there better deals around?

■ Have a look at any club memberships you hold: are you getting value for money?

That's just one example. You can apply the same principle of making lots of little changes to just about any aspect of life. The keys you can never find – start storing them consistently in the same place. The porch light you've been meaning to fix once you get a bulb – buy a few spares so that you're never caught short again. Update your virus checker. Start walking to work. Sell the CDs you no longer play.

'With ordinary talent and extraordinary perseverance, all things are attainable.'
THOMAS BOXWELL BUXTON (1786–1845), English social reformer

Defining idea...

Why not make a start by putting together a list of all the little things in your life that really irritate you? Then get cracking on making lots of those little improvements.

It's a great game for all the family as well. Asking the children for some ideas on how to improve the communal living experience, or just how to keep the house tidy, might throw up some pleasant surprises.

How did it go?

Q Isn't *kaizen* and all that quality stuff just a bit 1980s?

A   *Certainly, the whole quality movement is less fashionable now than then. Today, you don't get many CEOs talking about total quality as the way forward. It's the curse of anything that becomes fashionable that one day it will fall out of fashion. But the intelligent thinker doesn't throw babies out with bathwater. Kaizen was and is a useful concept and can add value. Perhaps the issue is more presentational than anything – use the principles of* kaizen *but change the label.*

Q Isn't there a danger of focusing on the small improvements so much that we lose the big picture? A bit like polishing the decks of the Titanic as the ship goes down.

A   *It isn't a matter of choosing to focus on either the small improvements or the big picture. We need to do both. The great thing about making small improvements is that everybody can be involved; that's rarely the case with the bigger, more strategic issues.*

17

Festina lente

No, not the latest addition to the coffee menu at Starbucks, but a piece of paradoxical advice in Latin that means 'Hurry slowly'. It's time to extol the tortoise mind and shackle the hare brain.

Ever found yourself rushing around trying to get something done in double-quick time, only to have some wag chirp up with the advice 'More haste, less speed'?

Tempting though it is to visit unimaginable violence on the head of this time-rich jerk, the little pest may actually have a point. We may live in the nanosecond noughties, but sometimes taking instant action doesn't get the best results.

It all, of course, comes down to the situation. If the microwave has just erupted into flames, then a period of languid contemplation about what to do for the best may not be the optimal strategy. Equally, there can be something about a rapidly looming deadline that concentrates the mind and really brings out the best in us. However, all too often, what we perceive to be quick thinking can mean glibness or superficiality.

Here's an idea for you...

Whenever you can, aim to become less timebound. For example, don't wear a watch unless you have to; let the phone just ring sometimes without answering it (that will put you one up on Pavlov's dogs); eat more slowly (hint: chew more before swallowing); walk as often as possible.

According to Guy Claxton, Visiting Professor of Learning Science at the University of Bristol, the human brain/mind can come up with any number of unusual, interesting and important insights if it is given the time. What Claxton terms the Tortoise Mind will often deliver a quiet, intuitive answer to questions and problems while its opposite number – the Hare Brain – is dashing frenetically and fruitlessly about.

The essence of tapping into our Tortoise Mind, then, is to recognise and accept that answers to some problems cannot be engineered, controlled or rushed in any way. This in itself offers a huge and fundamental challenge to the prevailing assumption nowadays that fast, purposeful thinking and more information are going to deliver answers to all our problems.

I suspect that intuitively we know this is right. How often have you found that pacing around trying to solve a problem by a concentrated force of intellectual willpower doesn't deliver the goods? Next time, try to allow yourself to forget about the problem for a while – go for a walk, turn your attention to something else, play the accordion, maybe even

sleep on it (no, not on the accordion – that would be a little bizarre). You may well find that the solution will pop fully formed into your head of its own accord.

Unfortunately, in a have-it-on-my-desk-by-lunchtime work and life culture, all too often the Tortoise Mind is starved of the time that it needs, and consequently its abilities are neglected. So in a world where the chips seem to be stacked heavily against the Tortoise Mind, what can we do to give slow and leisurely a fighting chance against fast and furious?

If you need a bit more urgency in your decision making, advance resolutely to IDEA 22, Make the best decision you can.

Try another idea...

For a start, we can decide to work to real rather than artificially concocted deadlines. My guess is that we have all been subjected to having to compile a report or similar for an organisational bigwig which 'absolutely must be on my desk first thing on Tuesday', only to discover that the report then languishes unread for days, maybe even weeks. So we should learn to challenge the deadlines that people give us, and in turn make sure that we don't inflict unnecessarily tight deadlines on others.

'A hibernation is a covert preparation for a more overt action.'
RALPH ELLISON

Defining idea...

We can also try to build more 'quiet reflection time' into our busy lives – pop into a local church at lunchtime, go for a stroll, listen to a calming piece of music, meditate and so on. A good chum of mine makes a tidy living out of outdoor coaching for stressed execs; he and the person being coached head off to the countryside and they spend a few hours walking, talking and reflecting, by all accounts with astonishing results.

'During periods of relaxation after concentrated intellectual activity, the intuitive mind seems to take over and can produce the sudden clarifying insights which give so much joy and delight.'
FRITJOF CAPRA

Defining idea...

Perhaps the key to success is for us to acknowledge and recognise that different problems require different approaches. The more complex the problem, the more likely it is that rushing to a quick solution could mean that we miss important details. Likewise, any questions that involve our emotional state are more likely to need the Tortoise Mind to mull things over.

How did it go?

Q I'm a bit concerned that letting my tortoise mind off the leash will get me labelled as a slowcoach and then I can see myself getting sacked for being so slow on the job. Can I afford to take the hard-shelled fellow into the workplace?

A I appreciate the problem. Some companies have an expectation that we will be pretty snappy thinkers in a cognitive sense. On the other hand, we need to recognise that we also have an emotional system, which is the basic regulatory system, and that works very slowly. You might call this our coping system. Part of the reason we need our tortoise mind is to help us cope with changing circumstances and priorities.

Q So the tortoise mind is our coping mechanism?

A Yes, that's true, though it does more as well. It's the source of our creative thinking. It's been labelled the intelligent unconscious in some quarters. It's where we mull over things before we consciously come to a conclusion. If organisations want us to be creative contributors in the workplace, they will have to place a positive value on our tortoise minds.

18

Kick-start your creativity

Are there times when your brain juices are not so much flowing as dribbling? Here are six suggestions for getting them positively gushing.

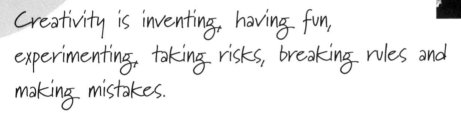

Creativity is inventing, having fun, experimenting, taking risks, breaking rules and making mistakes.

When we're on a creative roll, nothing seems easier or more natural. But when the ideas just aren't coming, we sometimes can't help wondering if we'll ever have another creative idea in our lives.

If you have ever wondered how to keep your creativity on tap so that a good idea is always there when needed, here are six suggestions:

CAPTURE YOUR IDEAS

Leonardo da Vinci always carried a notebook around with him so that he could capture any thoughts or ideas as they occurred. In his lifetime, he made around 14,000 pages of notes. Our best ideas often come to us when we're in a reasonably relaxed state – going to bed at the end of the day, while we're drifting in and out of sleep, when we're on a coach or a train and can afford to let our mind wander, or

Here's an idea for you...

When you're looking for your next good idea, be prepared to plagiarise, mix and match. As Albert Einstein said, the secret to creativity is knowing how to hide your sources. There are very few absolutely fresh and original ideas – most creative ideas are derived by extending existing ideas or by combining two or more familiar ideas. Let Google become your personal R&D department.

maybe even when we are at a particularly dull meeting! You can go down the da Vinci route of having a notebook constantly at your side, or you might prefer to use your laptop or PDA – the important thing is that you can harvest your ideas precisely as they occur.

CHANGE THE SCENERY

Extracting yourself from your normal day-to-day routines can be just the thing to prompt a creative idea or think something through. Here are some routine-breaking activities to consider:

- Go for a walk or bike ride
- Take a different route to or from work
- To gain some different perspectives, buy a magazine or a newspaper that you don't normally read
- Visit a museum or art gallery
- If you live in a city, visit the countryside (and vice versa)
- Go and sit down in a church or on a park bench for 20 minutes
- Watch some episodes of a favourite comedy series

FRAME THE QUESTION

Sometimes we are content to simply be alert to whatever ideas and inspirations come our way. That's fine as far as it goes, but if you have a particular problem you want to address, you need to have real clarity about what the problem actually is.

You can then use this clarity to frame a positive and focused challenge to yourself. So, for example, if the problem is that business is down 20 per cent, then you ask yourself a question along the lines of: What are all the ways in which we can increase the amount of business that we bring in?

Don't just create, innovate. For more on this, check IDEA 24, Innovate.

Try another idea...

DEVELOP YOUR IDEAS WITH A BUDDY

This works best when you're with somebody who's on your wavelength, somebody with whom you have an easy rapport. It's a bit of a cliché to say that two heads are better than one, but the fact is it all depends how well you get on with the other head! Don't edit your thinking or be afraid of saying something silly – some of the best ideas emerge when we're freewheeling. Get your buddy to test your thinking by asking some challenging questions. And remember to pick her brains as well.

'Curiosity has its own reason for existing.'
ALBERT EINSTEIN

Defining idea...

BE POSITIVE

Expect to get good ideas. Expect to come up with an answer. Use positive self-talk, such as phrases like 'I have excellent abilities', 'I see myself accomplishing my goals', 'I am an intelligent, talented person' and 'I have confidence in myself' (well it worked for Julie Andrews in *The Sound of Music*). If you create a positive atmosphere around you, it does rub off on others.

'An invasion of armies can be resisted, but not an idea whose time has come.'
VICTOR HUGO

Defining idea...

KEEP ALL CHANNELS OPEN

Pay particular heed to your intuition. As film director Frank Capra once said: a hunch is creativity trying to tell you something. Writer Robert Graves described intuition as 'the supra-logic that cuts out all the routine processes of thought and leaps straight from the problem to the answer'.

How did it go?

Q **I'm all for a bit of creativity, but shouldn't we really be concentrating a bit more on sticking to the knitting.**

A *There's a balance to be struck. There are certainly core activities that need to happen – whether we're talking about the workplace or the home. The biggest danger is that our main justification for doing things the way we do them is the fact that we've always done them that way. Times move on and we do need to keep at least an eye on our need to change with them.*

Q **I've just told my boss that I need to go to the museum to boost my creativity. He doesn't seem awfully taken with the idea. How can I persuade him?**

A *Companies are not always very comfortable with the implications of having a creative workforce. They tend sometimes to encourage creativity in their rhetoric but not in reality. You may need to find less challenging means of recharging your creative batteries. Alternatively, invite your boss to visit the museum with you – at lunchtime of course!*

19

De-junk your life

Overcrowding your work and home space can leave you feeling mentally overcrowded. Get rid of your physical clutter and your mental mess will sort itself out. Now where's that binliner?

If your home is anything like mine, it's awash with clutter. An off-the-cuff inspection of the premises earlier today revealed piles of CDs and DVDs, many of which I've never played, as well as books I've never read.

That's not to mention wedding presents that have never been used; more bikes than family members; the stamp collection I amassed as a lad; an old camera; a duelling sword; old LPs – yet strangely no turntable; a spare sofa; and some perfectly decent clothes into which my spreading girth will never again squeeze.

Before you scoff, take a look around your home and see if you come out any better.

Now I'm not suggesting you defect from the Clutter Junkies to join the Neat and Tidy Gang, but there's more to be gained from de-cluttering than just a few empty drawers and clean surfaces.

Here's an idea for you...

After you've tackled the physical clutter, have a crack at its psychic equivalent: all those tasks, jobs about the house and garden, and pet projects that have taken up permanent residence on your to-do list. Maybe the time has come to drop them, complete them, or give yourself a new and realistic deadline.

Clutter steals our attention, our time and our space. Clutter pushes many of us towards or deeper into debt. It makes us less efficient, as we forever misplace house keys, bills and slips of paper bearing important telephone numbers. The visual distraction caused by clutter can make it more difficult to concentrate.

Most psychologists agree that a messy home environment can exert a negative, though not immediately obvious, influence on a child's cognitive and emotional development. Young children learn and develop to best effect in environments that are ordered, consistent and understandable. Put simply, it's more difficult to learn in chaotic and cluttered surroundings.

Things don't get much better when we grow up. Although we persuade ourselves that we can rise above our physical surroundings no matter how chaotic, scientific research shows that the vast majority of us perform tasks more quickly and to a higher standard when we undertake them in a structured and tidy environment.

For those who are wallowing in a clutter bath, here are a few tips on how to banish mess from your life:

- Start gradually: work on a single drawer, cupboard or small area that would benefit from a clearout. If you want to go for broke, copy your CDs and old vinyl onto your computer and either store them out of sight or sell them.

- Appreciate the difference between having a clearout and getting organised – one is not the inevitable consequence of the other. When (and only when) you've finished dejunking, then start to put what's left into some kind of order. Get hold of some filing cabinets or storage units; buy some albums for your loose photos.

You can extend decluttering to other parts of your life by checking out some principles of brain-friendly, healthy eating at IDEA 35, *From Masterchef to Mastermind – eat your way to genius.*

Try another idea...

- Change what you don't like – those curtains you've always hated, the threadbare carpet, the doorknob that's forever coming off in your hands. Your surroundings should inspire you, not frustrate or irritate you.

- Take a few minutes at the end of each day to put things in order – at work, at home, in your car – so that you can start fresh the next day.

- Take all your unwanted stuff to a car boot sale or post it on the cyberspace equivalent – eBay: aside from the ominous feng shui implications of this clutter, there are real financial benefits to be gained from minimising the stuff we have to provide space for, take care of and insure. It's said to be better to give than to receive; here, it's often better to sell than to keep. And think of all the ways you could spend the money.

'I'm a natural prey for the 3for2 offer. Like a lot of people I am assembling a great archive to bequeath to my children who won't watch them either.'
CHARLIE HIGSON, novelist, comedian and scriptwriter

Defining idea...

The other thing to watch out for is clutter creepback; bit by bit, the clutter can return as you buy more books, CDs, magazines and general stuff for the house. We all need to stay clutter vigilant!

How did it go?

Q **I had a go at decluttering and ended up taking over a hundred books to a local charity shop. Now I find there's a book that I gave away that I really want to read again. Did I go too far?**

A *Not necessarily. If it was a book you've read and re-read over the years, perhaps you should have hung on to it. Otherwise, I'd suggest that you think about the space saved by the 99 books you will probably never want to see again rather than harp on about going a book too far with your clearout. You can always buy another copy or, better still, borrow it from somebody.*

Q **OK, I've finished my clearout. Am I done?**

A *Have you really finished? What about your collection of vinyl records that you can't play any more because you don't have a turntable? What about copying all your CDs onto your computer and/or your iPod? This may be a morbid thought, but imagine you've just died and your relatives have come to clear the house. How much of your stuff would they put straight in a skip? Perhaps there is scope for being a bit more ruthless.*

20

What did the Greeks ever do for us?

How to entice other people to your point of view. Aristotle offered three methods of convincing others: through logic, through character or reputation, and through the emotions.

Go back more than two thousand years and, if there were a competition for persuasive philosophers, a Greek would be world champion.

Aristotle (384–322 BC) is just about the most famous of the ancient philosophers. More than any other philosopher, he shaped the orientation of Western intellectual history by integrating methods of formal logic into a system of thought.

Aristotle proposed that there were three elements that could be deployed in constructing and presenting an argument to an audience, namely logos (focused on logic), ethos (focused on the character or reputation of the speaker) and pathos (focused on appeal to and through the emotions). Yes, I know they sound a bit like the Three Musketeers, but let's just look at each in turn to see how they can help us improve our ability to persuade others to our point of view.

Here's an idea for you...

Start tracking the extent to which you use logos, ethos and pathos when you're trying to bring somebody around to your point of view. And listen out for how other people use the three. Different people respond better to different approaches. If you rely on pathos to persuade somebody who uses a lot of logos in their conversations, you're mismatching. Try to find the common ground.

LOGOS

Logos is the study of the principles and methods involved in constructing valid and logical arguments.

Here is an example of a valid argument:

A   All politicians are shifty.
B   Tony Blair is a politician.
C   (Therefore) Tony Blair is shifty.

This form of argument is called a syllogism, and is an example of deductive logic. It's worth noting that we can only draw the logical conclusion that 'Tony Blair is shifty' because statement A talks about 'all' politicians. Likewise, if statement A had stated that 'no politicians are shifty', then we could logically conclude that Tony Blair is not shifty.

If the statement was that 'most' politicians are shifty, then we could not logically conclude that C is definitely the case. That said, if we applied inductive logic, we could conclude that because most politicians are shifty, it is possible, perhaps even probable, that Tony Blair is shifty.

IDEA 4, _Get to the point_, provides more useful tips on putting across your message effectively.

Try another idea...

ETHOS

Ethos is concerned with the degree of credibility or trustworthiness that speakers or writers have in the eyes of their audience. Where the speaker's character is viewed favourably by the audience, this is seen as giving value to the ideas in the argument, whereas the same speech delivered by somebody of disreputable character might well be viewed unfavourably. Think Nelson Mandela, then think Jeffrey Archer or Martha Stewart and you'll probably get the hang of this.

PATHOS

Pathos is concerned with persuading an audience by arousing their emotions. Here's an example of pathos in action: it's a short section from a speech given by Richard Nixon at the 1952 Republican Convention when he was chosen to be Eisenhower's running mate. Known as Nixon's 'Checkers Speech', it was widely regarded as a political triumph.

'It is the mark of an educated mind to be able to entertain a thought without accepting it.'
ARISTOTLE

Defining idea...

'We did get something – a gift – after the election.
A man down in Texas heard Pat on the radio mention the fact that our two
youngsters would like to have a dog. And, believe it or not, the day before we left
on this campaign trip we got a message from Union Station in Baltimore saying they
had a package for us. We went down to get it. You know what it was?

It was a little cocker spaniel dog in a crate that he'd sent all the way from Texas.
Black and white spotted. And our little girl – Tricia, the 6-year-old – named it
Checkers. And you know, the kids, like all kids, love the dog and I just want to say
this right now, that regardless of what they say about it, we're gonna keep it.'

Ah, bless. You can just imagine that audience of Republicans coming over all soppy
and smiling benignly at each other as they fell hook, line and sinker for Tricky
Dickie's piece of manipulative hokum.

Still, I shouldn't mock. Although Aristotle believed that logos was the most
important element in any argument, and that ethos and pathos were subsidiary
elements, there's some evidence to suggest that nowadays it's logos in bronze
position, with pathos taking the silver and ethos the gold.

That's something worth remembering the next time you're on the stump.

86

Q **I tried mentioning Aristotle to my acquaintances and they seem to think he is a Brazilian footballer! How can I persuade them to accept all this logos, pathos and ethos stuff?**

How did it go?

A *Think what Mary Poppins would do in this situation. She'd be using the spoonful of sugar technique. If people don't like the language, change the language. Don't talk about logos, pathos and ethos, talk about logical argument, personal credibility and emotional investment. And don't even mention Aristotle – he's been dead for centuries so is unlikely to take offence.*

Q **I've just given a presentation using these three elements. Although my logical arguments were fine and I put the necessary amount of emotion into the talk, it seemed that people doubted my credibility to talk on the subject. Anything I can do about this?**

A *Credibility is the trickiest of the three to achieve. Once you have a reputation in a field, it tends to stick unless you do something spectacular to lose it. If you don't appear to have it already, it will take time to gain it. Sometimes, though, the problem is that a certain group of people have known you for years and have already labelled you; if you make the same presentation to strangers they'll be much more likely to take your credibility as read.*

21

It's good to talk

Read on for chapter and verse on how you can talk and write yourself into lucidity.

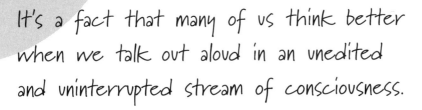

It's a fact that many of us think better when we talk out aloud in an unedited and uninterrupted stream of consciousness.

So own up, have you ever broken somebody else's thought flow by perpetrating any of the following:

- Interrupted somebody who was speaking before that person had finished making a point?

- Interrupted somebody even before the end of a sentence?

- Jumped in and started speaking as soon as there was the slightest pause in the conversation?

- Jumped in and finished off the speaker's sentence, assuming you knew how it was going to end?

- Not responded to the point made by the speaker but instead started an entirely new thread of conversation?

Here's an idea for you...

A good tool for capturing your stream-of-consciousness thoughts and ideas is to get into the habit of journaling. Buy a notebook and every morning – preferably as soon as you get up – set aside 20–30 minutes to write two or three pages of anything that comes to mind. This could be problems you encountered the day before, ideas, dreams, rambling thoughts and so on. It's a curious experience. Initially, you'll find yourself writing about fairly trivial stuff ('feeling a bit crap today', 'it's raining', 'think I'll have muesli for breakfast'), but you can quickly find yourself exploring some fairly deep terrain.

- Looked to the speaker as though you were about to do one of the above, thereby causing the speaker to either lose her train of thought or hurry to make her point?

I suspect the real question is not so much 'have you ever' done any of the above, but 'how many times today' have you done these things. It's as though we're all battling away in a little-known subset of Darwinian theory called 'the survival of the chattiest'.

There are some who say that this competition for airtime is just a sign of our chat-tastic times, that there's little that can be done about it and, besides, there's nothing wrong with a bit of conversational cut-and-thrust. The problem is that sometimes we need a bit of thinking time in order to nurture our thoughts. We can't always rattle off our thoughts and opinions on every subject as though our brain is a library of fully formed soundbites.

I have a friend who maintains that she often doesn't know what she's really thinking and feeling until she's voiced her thoughts aloud. I suspect that now and again we could all use an opportunity to tease out our thoughts and talk ourselves into lucidity.

So here's a suggestion – give yourself time to think by giving yourself time to talk. To that end, when there is something that you want to talk your way through, invite somebody suitable to be your thinking buddy. They don't have to say anything when you're talking; on the contrary, their role is to stay silent while you are speaking. They just have to listen and look interested.

If you can talk yourself into lucidity, you might have an aptitude for telling stories. See IDEA 37, *Become an ace storyteller.*

Try another idea...

You might be wondering what value a non-speaking buddy adds to the whole process. Technically, of course, you could begin a thinking session by just talking aloud when you're on your own. However, many people find this quite difficult to do in practice, and prefer to have somebody else in the room to make the process a little more natural. You will also get non-verbal feedback about the sense you are making, either positive (eyes open, sitting up straight) or negative (eyes closed, body slumped and evidence of dribble).

If time is an issue, agree a time-limit for the session. You might find that your thinking buddy has something to think through too. There's actually a nice sense of receiving and returning the favour when you both have a go.

Some of my more battle-hardened, I-didn't-get-where-I-am-today-by-listening-to people chums are a bit sceptical about all this. One mate in particular dismissed the idea as cushion-hugging, namby-pamby nonsense. Then he gave it a go – and changed his mind.

'Work increasingly consists of talk...There are very few supreme heights left where you need listen only to your own voice.'
THEODORE ZELDIN, international thought leader

Defining idea...

That said, these thinking sessions may not be everybody's cup of tea. My advice would be to find an hour in your diary, give it a go and see how you get on. Then at least you'll know.

How did it go?

Q I got somebody to be my listening buddy but it seemed very odd that they said so little. Are you sure I'm doing it right?

A The presence of another person makes it much more natural for us to talk aloud, but their role is not to grill us like the Spanish Inquisition; rather, they should simply to listen to us and pay attention. Apart from kicking off the thinking session by asking what you want to think about, your thinking partner should say next to nothing. Just having somebody else with us improves our ability to think.

Q So how would you sell the benefits of talking yourself into lucidity to somebody who had never tried it?

A I'd tell the person this: having a thinking session means that you have that rare gift – uninterrupted thinking time. You can repeat yourself, deviate and hesitate as much as you like – you know you won't be cut off in your thinking prime. When the signs are that you've said your piece, your buddy can ask you whether there's anything else you want to say. If there isn't, that's the end of the session. Quite often, though, you'll find that you pause...and then start talking again. Just because you stopped talking, it doesn't necessarily mean that you've stopped thinking. So it's useful if your buddy holds back from jumping in until they pick up a clear signal that you want them to.

22

Make the best decision you can

People can spend months debating the 'best' decision without actually deciding anything. Here are some pointers to good decision making. Turns out it's often a teams and timing thing.

Like good comedy, the key to good decision making is (pause) timing. Give yourself time to think, but don't procrastinate.

Before we get going, let's knock on the head the notion that 'being decisive' and 'making good decisions' are necessarily the same thing.

Let's remember that Margaret Thatcher was the model of a decisive Prime Minister, and that President George Bush is regarded as a firm decision maker. Yet both have made some whopping errors of judgement – for example, introducing the poll tax in Thatcher's case, and as for Bush, well there are just too many poorly thought through débâcles to choose from (allegedly).

So it's clear that being overly decisive can often as not turn out badly. Of course, the same can be true of those people who are the opposite – underly decisive, as it

Here's an idea for you...

Practice making some 'just-in-time' decisions – neither premature and thus risking not having the necessary evidence, nor too late and thus missing the boat. Do this by making your decision as late as possible – but before you need to take action.

were. Unnecessary procrastination often leads to results every bit as bad as those gained by the obsessively decisive. Think of all the appeasers in history who were just that bit too inclined to do nothing, arguing instead the merits of giving the benefit of the doubt to a rank wrong 'un. When you have to make a choice and you back off from making it, that itself is a choice (ah, those years spent in philosophy class weren't entirely wasted).

Decision making can be defined as the ability to decide on a course of action after due reflection. Good decision makers seem to have three key abilities, namely to:

1. gather the appropriate evidence (and, equally, to ignore the irrelevant or immaterial evidence)
2. weigh up the evidence correctly
3. make the decision at just the right time, i.e. neither too early nor too late

Sometimes decision making is a solo pastime – perhaps nobody else is around, or maybe it's just inappropriate to involve others because the decision isn't that complex or important, or possibly you are the only person with all the necessary information to be able to make that decision.

Defining idea...

'A good plan implemented today is better than a perfect plan implemented tomorrow.'
GEORGE S. PATTON

On other occasions, we can reach a better quality decision by involving others. In his book *The Wisdom of Crowds*, *New Yorker* columnist James Surowiecki explores how large groups of people can consistently deploy their pooled wisdom to outstrip individuals – no matter how brilliant the individual – at solving problems, fostering innovation and coming to wise decisions.

If you want to know more about how to avoid making bad decisions, have a look at IDEA 28, *Caught in a decision trap.*

Try another idea...

Of course, it's not always appropriate to resolve decisions by committee, but there is evidence to show that, when presented with almost any problem, a group will consistently outperform an individual in terms of identifying the relevant factors to consider, gaining the knowledge possessed about those factors and accurately weighing up the evidence.

When it comes to making the decision at the right time, there is obviously no 'one-size-fits-all' point at which this optimal moment presents itself. Every decision has to be assessed in its own context. Generally speaking, you'll find it's more important to make the right decision than the 'best' decision. Every decision involves a level of risk, and some decisions are more critical than others to get absolutely right.

'When making a decision of minor importance, I have always found it advantageous to consider all the pros and cons. In vital matters, however, such as the choice of a mate or a profession, the decision should come from the unconscious, from somewhere within ourselves.'
SIGMUND FREUD

Defining idea...

But if there are a number of ways of doing something, and it looks like most of them would work well enough, there's little value to be gained – and much time to be lost – in agonising over finding the best possible solution. On those occasions, just be pragmatic: implement a perfectly satisfactory solution – even if it's not absolutely optimal – and then rapidly move on to the next problem.

Q **Before I read this Idea I was decisive, but now I'm not so sure. Is that really a good outcome?**

A *Being decisive is intrinsically neither a bad quality nor a good one. If we look at the origins of the verb 'to decide', it turns out that it stems from the Latin meaning 'to kill off'. When we make a decision, we are 'killing off' other choices. So it's important that we make the decision at the right time with as much evidence as we can muster. Good decision makers are decisive when the time comes to be decisive. Bad decision makers are often guilty of premature decisiveness.*

Q **I was out with a group of mates last night and we just couldn't agree where we wanted to go to eat. Isn't there an argument for having a strong leader saying 'this is what we are going to do' and saving a whole lot of time and aggravation?**

A *Achieving consensus can be a time-consuming business, so it's not always the appropriate decision-making method. If a fire breaks out somewhere, you wouldn't want the crew at a fire station to debate whether they should attend the incident or not; you'd want them to just leap into action. But the point is that anybody working in the fire service has previously consented to operating on that basis. You can apply the same principle to deciding where to eat. One person might decide on behalf of the group, and that will work as long as the group had previously agreed that was the way to make the decision.*

23

Take a walk on the Wilde side

If you've ever thought of the perfect riposte but found that the moment for delivering it has long gone, this one is for you.

Ever had the experience of coming up with the perfect witty riposte to a remark but, alas, coming up with it too late to deliver it?

The remark might have occurred to you the morning after or it might just be a matter of seconds too late. Whatever. The point is that the perfect moment to casually toss off your verbal Exocet has gone. Your razor-sharp wit is rendered as blunt as Simon Cowell in a grumpy mood confronted with a tone-deaf, charisma-free non-entity.

It will probably come as little consolation that the French, as is their wont, have a phrase for this phenomenon. They call it *l'esprit d'escalier*, literally the spirit of the staircase, to register the point that we tend to think of these ripostes after we have left the scene.

Here's an idea for you... **Improve your ability to think on the hoof by join a debating society, a book club or any forum where you have to exchange views 'real time'. If you can track one down in your neck of the woods, consider signing up for a stand-up comedy workshop.**

So why can't we be more of a spontaneous wit like (insert your chosen name – Stephen Fry, Robin Williams, Eddie Izzard, Peter Ustinov, or whoever)?

Most people who knew him believed that Oscar Wilde was the best conversationalist and most witty person that they'd ever met. George Bernard Shaw called Wilde 'the greatest talker of his time, perhaps of all time'. Sir Max Beerbohm – who had met renowned wits like Henry James, G.K. Chesterton and Hilaire Belloc – maintained that none of them was in Wilde's league. 'Oscar in his own way was the greatest of them all,' Beerbohm once said, 'the most spontaneous and yet the most polished, the most soothing and yet the most surprising.'

So we could make a solid case for arguing that Oscar Wilde represents the gold standard of spontaneous wits. If we were re-engineering our riposte capability, Oscar would be our benchmark. Anybody taking on Wilde in a verbal exchange would probably win as many points as Long John Silver would manage in a tennis match against Roger Federer.

Being witty is one thing, being able to hold a good conversation is another. Check out IDEA 41, *Be a first-class conversationalist* for some tips.

Try another idea...

So what was the secret of Oscar's success? Well the truth is that, like Disraeli, Churchill and others famed for their spontaneous wit, Wilde's wit was the result of careful preparation rather than spontaneity. He would enter into conversations, pre-loaded with sparkling observations and simply wait for the right moment to deliver them.

Sometimes, apparently, his patience snapped and he engineered conversational gambits that would set up a witticism he was particularly keen to deliver. Once, for example, he asked an acquaintance about his religious convictions, provoking a sincere and serious response. When the acquaintance had finished speaking, Wilde said with a smile, 'You are so evidently, so unmistakably sincere and most of all so truthful, that...I can't believe a single word you say.'

At this point, you might like to start reappraising some of your supposedly spontaneous comedic icons. Take Morecambe and Wise, for example, who were rightly renowned for comic performances that verged on the edge on chaos, performances that were jam-packed with apparently unplanned moments and off-the-cuff remarks. They were a pair of comic geniuses, without a doubt, but it was pretty much all in the script. The same goes for the Marx Brothers.

'Quotation is a serviceable substitute for wit.'
OSCAR WILDE

Defining idea...

I'm not trying to argue that spontaneous wit doesn't exist, just that (i) it's not as common as we might think; and (ii) it is possible to fake it. How we do that is by building up our stockpile of pre-honed witticisms so that, like Wilde, we can use them as the opportunity arises. That stockpile might be our own homemade efforts or it might just as effectively be culled from others. In the heat of a conversation, very few people will spot that your witty remark was nicked from an old Bob Hope movie.

As you become more accomplished and confident, you might want to try engineering conversations in the direction of your ready-and-waiting bon mot.

To that end, I'd like to leave you at this point with a few contributions to help get your pre-crafted library of spontaneous wit off the ground. They're not great, but at least it's a start:

I'd like to help you out. Which way did you come in?

I'm busy now. Can I ignore you some other time?

If ignorance is bliss, you must be the happiest person alive.

Mmmm, you can see why I don't need them anymore.

Defining
idea... **'Wit is educated insolence.'**
ARISTOTLE

Q **I've had a go at coming up in advance with some witty remarks. When I said them, I got no reaction at all. Why not?**

How did it go?

A *A handbag?*

Q **Pardon?**

A *The key point about being witty is your use of context and timing. 'A handbag?' is a classic line from Oscar Wilde's* The Importance of Being Earnest, *but it's only funny when it fits into a particular conversational context. Or perhaps you got your timing wrong. Start watching comedians on the TV or listening to them on the radio and you'll find that most of them will make use of short pauses to heighten comic effect. A semi-pro friend of mine talks about how people can kill the impact of an amusing remark by what he calls 'premature e-joke-ulation' – delivering a punchline in too hurried a fashion. Of course there is another possibility. Perhaps your 'witty remarks' just weren't funny.*

Q **A handbag?**

A *Very good. Shall we move on?*

24

Innovate

In an ever more unpredictable world, success goes inevitably to people who have a natural curiosity and who are willing to experiment. Assuming that what works today will still work tomorrow is a recipe for the scrapheap.

Michael Eisner, former Head of the Disney Corporation and a big fan of innovative thinking, once said: 'To me, the pursuit of ideas is the only thing that matters. You can always find capable people to do almost anything else.'

Successful innovation – whether for a company or for us in our private lives – requires a conscious and explicit commitment and inevitably involves risk. It is best achieved in a 'no blame' culture, which recognises that mistakes and failures are the natural and inevitable bedfellows of successful ideas. An innovative organisation is typically characterised by informality, the free flow of information, and little hierarchy or bureaucracy.

Ask naive questions that test people's assumptions. A simple yet explicit question like 'So why do we do it this way?' is a great way of revealing that, actually, the way things are done currently is often more a matter of habit than anything else.

Here are a few tips that will help to hone your capability in this area:

Continually challenge conventional wisdom

Question all the time. Don't be impressed by precedent. Regularly ask yourself how else you could do this, or what you would do differently if you could start again from scratch.

Listen to other people's views

Learn from the experience of others. Draw on their intuition and common sense. Encourage ideas from others. Benchmark other departments, other organisations.

Disagree constructively

Innovation depends on relentless self-questioning and the pursuit of continual improvement through constructive argument.

Seek out new experiences

Travel to a new country. Go into a newsagent, buy a handful of magazines outside of your area of expertise, read what's going on in other fields and see if you can make any connections back to your working environment. Try a secondment to another part of the business.

Join cross-functional teams whenever you get the chance

Many problems are best solved by inter-disciplinary thinking. Perhaps it's time to meet up with those people from production, finance, marketing and human resources (ah, the sacrifices we must make...).

Network voraciously

Share your ideas, and see what reaction you get. Meet up with people who share your interests – fellow professionals, local clubs, etc. – on a regular basis.

Innovation is about thinking outside of the box. It might help to become a master of paradox. Try **IDEA 38,** *What is the sound of one hand clapping?*

Try another idea...

Capture accidents

Remember that, sometimes, getting the wrong answer is as enlightening as getting the right answer. Many of the greatest inventions were accidental – the Post-It note, for example.

Fail often

It's supposed to have taken Thomas Edison 10,000 attempts to perfect the invention of the lightbulb. Getting things wrong from time to time shows that you're entrepreneurial and willing to take risks. It's not evidence of moral turpitude.

GSOH

Show others that you have a good sense of humour. Encourage it in others. Remember that many of the best ideas from brainstorming sessions start off as funny remarks.

'I can't understand why people are frightened of new ideas. I'm frightened of the old ones.'
JOHN CAGE, composer

Defining idea...

Wait until the last minute

Delay making judgements. Postpone criticism.
Keep an open mind. It's uncanny how many good ideas turn up in the nick of time.

Defining
idea...

'By definition, risk-takers often fail. So do morons. In practice it's difficult to sort them out.'
SCOTT ADAMS

Be willing to change your mind

Holding stubbornly to a point of view is not a sign of strength. The best innovators are prepared to admit that they are wrong sometimes.

...and relax

Take advantage of coffee breaks, cab rides and other opportunities for a few minutes' downtime. Innovative ideas often come in places and at times that can surprise us. If you can, sleep on a problem – solutions regularly pop up after a few hours' kip.

A word of warning. It's all very well being innovative in an environment that encourages and supports innovation. Being innovative in an unsupportive environment, for example a risk-averse life assurance company, is difficult and occasionally downright dangerous. The innovative pragmatists in those types of organisation might well decide to suppress their creative instincts, keep their heads down for a bit, and return to being their natural selves come the next change of job.

Q **I've tried talking to people around me about the need to innovate, but I'm not really comfortable with the word itself – it seems too grandiose. What else can I call it?**

How did it go?

A *There are plenty of other words you can use which sound a little less daunting. You can talk about 'making changes', 'coming up with some new ideas', 'introducing new ways of doing things' and so on if you prefer.*

Q **I'm getting a lot of resistance to the idea of innovation. People keep asking me how important is it anyway, and in reality does it need to happen that often?**

A *You can tell them that it depends on the context. When people at Disney talk about the need to innovate, they are working in an explicitly creative environment and so innovation is absolutely essential. For anyone working in a more down-to-earth environment, innovation may be neither wanted nor needed on a day-to-day basis. However, wherever we work or whatever we do, it's always useful to question whether the current formula is still working. If there are suspicions that it isn't, then the time may well be ripe for some innovative thinking.*

107

25

Manoeuvre like Machiavelli

You may find yourself pitting your wits against the Machiavellian mindset from time to time so it might help to know what you're up against. Alternatively, if you're a closet admirer, you might pick up a few tips.

If Nicolo Machiavelli inhabited the twenty-first century rather than sixteenth-century Italy, he would surely recognise a political world often driven more by resolute pragmatism than morality.

That his book *The Prince* is still in print more than 500 years after it was written reflects the timelessness of its content. Its main theme, that princes should retain absolute control of their territories and should use any means of expediency to accomplish this end, as well as many of his insights into the nature of leadership and strategy, would get a hearty nod of approval from many of today's politicians and senior managers.

Over the years, Machiavelli's extremely pragmatic view of the relationship between ethics and politics has been widely misinterpreted. His surname, of course, has generated an adjective that is a byword for people who prefer expediency to morality, and who manipulate others in an opportunistic and deceptive way.

Here's an idea for you...

Spend the next few hours really listening to what people say and ask yourself whether what they say is what they mean. Often, the subtext carries the real message more than what's actually said. For example, when somebody asks their partner if they are planning to get changed before going out that evening, is it a genuine, open question or is there a hidden message along the lines of 'You're not going out looking like that, are you?'

This isn't altogether fair on Machiavelli: yes, he advocated deploying the darker side of human nature to achieve the desired goals, but only when, as he put it, 'necessity commands'.

MINING THE MACHIAVELLIAN MINDSET

The Prince is a book that is more talked about than actually read. So let's delve into Machiavelli's classic to highlight some of the more controversial aspects of his analysis. Here are some of his key points:

Machiavelli describes how some 'virtues' will lead to a prince's destruction, whereas some 'vices' allow him to survive. Indeed, the virtues that we commonly praise in people might lead to a prince's downfall. Although we might think that it is best for a prince to have a reputation of being generous, Machiavelli writes that 'liberality exercised in a way that does not bring you the reputation for it, injures you'.

It is wiser, according to Machiavelli, to have a reputation for meanness than generosity because that brings 'reproach without hatred'.

It is better for a prince to be severe when punishing people rather than merciful. Severity through death sentences affects only a few, but it deters crimes which affects many. Further, he argues, it is better to be feared than to be loved.

In perhaps the most controversial section of *The Prince*, Machiavelli argues that the prince should know how to be deceitful when it suits his purpose. When the prince needs to be deceitful, though, he must not appear that way. Indeed, he must always exhibit five particular virtues: mercy, honesty, humaneness, uprightness and religiousness.

To understand more about how others try to manipulate us, move along to IDEA 34, *Trust me – I'm a salesman*. Go on then.

Try another idea…

Machiavelli argues that the prince must avoid doing things which will cause him to be hated. This is accomplished by not confiscating property, and not appearing greedy or wishy-washy. In fact, the best way to avoid being overthrown is to avoid being hated.

'I have a cunning plan.'
BALDRICK in *Blackadder I* (and *II*, *III* and *IV*)

Defining idea…

It's important for the smart thinker to understand the Machiavellian mindset because it's alive and kicking. You only have to look at the behaviour of many governments and organisations to see that realpolitik is alive and kicking. We might criticise people like George Bush for their stance on…well just about everything, but the fact is they are *über*-pragmatists driven by self-interest – not unlike Machiavelli's prince. And like all pragmatists, they 'just don't get' arguments that are presented from a theoretical or ethical base.

If that's where you naturally come from, then you need to change your game plan to convince a pragmatic opponent that your suggestions can satisfy their self-interest.

'The essence of lying is in deception, not in words.'
JOHN RUSKIN

Defining idea…

Equally, if you are a pragmatist by nature dealing with a values-driven opponent, you may also need to adjust your tone so that you can appeal to their moral sensibilities. But then again, if you are a pragmatist, that shouldn't cause you too many problems, should it?

How did it go?

Q **I've tried to get into the Machiavellian mindset but I'm not at all comfortable about it. The idea of setting out to manipulate the behaviour of others is abhorrent to me. Need I continue?**

A *Your feelings are understandable. Perhaps, instead, you should focus on developing your ability to spot when others are trying to manipulate you. There are plenty of pragmatists out there who take the view that 'necessity commands' and it's as well to be aware that other people don't have your value base.*

Q **Is there any kind of half-way house here? Is it possible to combine pragmatism with holding strong personal values?**

A *The two can work together. Some people with strong value sets can be extremely pragmatic in cajoling people to do 'the right thing'. Bob Geldof is probably a master of this. It's less clear that a pragmatist could hold strong values, although Groucho Marx did once once remark that if you could fake sincerity, then you've got it made!*

26

Feed your head

Blimey, it turns out that the fast track to boosting your brainpower is sex and drugs and rock 'n' roll. Not to mention kip 'n' grub. Result!

How many parents have ever told their errant offspring that people get what they deserve in life?

It turns out that there are five key areas where we can boost the performance of our grey matter without having to slave away at it too much. They are:

1. Physical exercise
2. Smart drugs
3. Music on the brain

4. Sleep on it
5. Food for thought

Here's an idea for you... **Contact your doctor over the next week or two and book yourself a physical check-up if you haven't had one for a while. This should include getting readings for blood pressure, cholesterol and body mass index. Then put together a 'better health' action plan for you to follow over the coming months.**

PHYSICAL EXERCISE

Researchers have found that simply walking at a reasonably relaxed pace three times a week for half an hour can boost abilities such as learning, concentration and abstract reasoning by around 15 per cent. Having sex can achieve similar benefits.

There are two reasons why aerobic exercise is good for our mental performance: exercise gets extra oxygen into our brains; and it also promotes the growth of new brain cells.

Older people particularly benefit from exercise. Pensioners who walk regularly outperform their sedentary peers in memory tests. What's more, exercise can help slow the decline in their scores on various cognitive tests relative to non-walkers.

THE DRUGS DO WORK

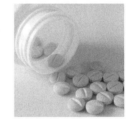

There are a number of drugs on the market – known as 'cognitive enhancers' – with more on the way. Modafinil, for example, is licensed to treat narcolepsy, but it also has notable effects on healthy people as well. Modafinil can keep you awake and alert for up to 90 hours straight, with none of the side effects like jitteriness and bad concentration that amphetamines or coffee can produce. What's more, sleep-deprived people taking modafinil can outperform their unmedicated peers who have had a good night's sleep.

The next wave of drugs – some of which have been designed explicitly to boost memory – are now going through clinical trials.

For more on the importance of **a good eating regime, waddle over to IDEA 35,** *From Masterchef to Mastermind – eat your way to genius.*

Try another idea...

MUSIC ON THE BRAIN

Listening to music – and Mozart in particular, it seems – can improve people's mathematical and spatial reasoning. Listening to music can relax and stimulate us simultaneously, and it's this combination that enables us to perform some activities more effectively.

There's also evidence that taking music lessons can make us smarter. A study of young children found that those taking music lessons benefited from a 2–3 per cent hike in their IQ scores relative to their peer group.

'I hate people who think it's clever to take drugs...like customs officers.'
JACK DEE, British comedian

Defining idea...

SLEEP ON IT

Sleep helps the brain consolidate memories and hone skills so that they are readily available during waking hours. There's also plenty of evidence to show that sleep provides an opportunity for the brain to work through problems that we haven't managed to crack during our waking hours. A good night's sleep improves our ability to concentrate the next day.

Even a short burst of sleep can help. Napping for an hour or two before an exam improves performance (sadly, napping for an hour or two during the exam doesn't).

FOOD FOR THOUGHT

When it comes to having an appetite, the brain is the Billy Bunter of organs, far and away the greediest organ in your body.

Eating breakfast makes a very sensible first fuel-stop of the day. Even having a piece of toast has been shown to boost children's scores in a range of cognitive tests, more so if accompanied by something with high protein and decent fibre – we're talking baked beans, for example. You might not be the most popular person in class on this sort of diet, but who cares, you're going to Oxford! If you can't enthuse over eating beans, wholemeal toast and Marmite will give you a decent academic shunt.

Paying attention to each of these five key areas will help you achieve a better performance in your work and home life. And let's be honest, there's no great hardship involved.

So come on then, let's look to boost our performance the twenty-first-century way: no need for hours of study – just walk or jog home, rustle up a piece of toast, pop a few pills, put in a bit of practice on the electric guitar and then grab a few hours sleep.

Q **Eat well, sleep well, don't drink too much, and take some exercise when you can. Isn't this all just common sense?**

How did it go?

A *Mostly, yes, although many people have noted that there's often a big gap between common sense and common practice. We might know the rudiments of sensible living, but we don't always abide by good practice.*

Q **OK, I'm doing all the right things, and even listening to the right music. I'm just a bit worried about the apparent advocacy of these 'cognitive enhancers'. Are they really a necessary part of the mix?**

A *It remains to be seen. In the sporting world, most of us would regard any drug that confers a physical advantage as 'cheating'; we've yet to have the same debate about drugs that improve our mental performance. What is clear is that cognitive enhancers are in the drugs approval pipeline and will soon be coming onto the market as legally available substances. But it's anybody's guess what happens in the future when one child on enhancers gets better exam results than a similarly able child who doesn't use these supplements. It rather undermines the whole qualification system.*

117

27

Let's hear it for the poise

It's not enough to be intelligent these days; you need to be emotionally intelligent as well. For a look at what that entails, please read on.

Here's a favourite quote of mine — it was made by a supermarket till operator: 'Management says that we don't have to say thank you any more because the computer prints it on the receipt.'

Funny, yet strangely disturbing, and a reminder – as if it were needed – that, in many places, emotional intelligence is more noticeable by its absence than its shining presence.

WHAT EXACTLY IS EMOTIONAL INTELLIGENCE?

According to Daniel Goleman, the main populariser of the concept, it is the capacity for recognising our own feelings and those of others, for motivating ourselves and for managing emotions well in ourselves and in our relationships with other people.

Here's an idea for you... **Spend the next few days watching how different people handle emotional flashpoints – parents with their children, shop workers dealing with complaining customers and so on. Notice what the emotionally intelligent say and do to resolve problems compared with those who lack skills in this area. It's so much easier to learn from real life examples than from words on a page.**

Goleman believes that emotional intelligence embraces five emotional and social competencies:

Self-awareness: knowing what we are feeling at the moment and using those preferences to guide our decision-making.

Self-management: handling our emotions so that they facilitate rather than interfere with the task in hand. This enables us to respond thoughtfully and intelligently to situations rather than merely to react.

Motivation: through self-awareness, using our deepest preferences to move and guide us toward our goals. This involves understanding what makes us 'tick' – what we respond positively to and what doesn't work for us.

Empathy: sensing what others are feeling, being able to take their perspective and being able to cultivate good, positive rapport with a broad range of people.

Relationship management: handling emotions in relationships well and accurately reading social situations and networks; interacting smoothly; using these skills to persuade, lead, negotiate and settle disputes, etc. True emotional intelligence is about dealing with people's behaviour, not labelling the person behind that behaviour.

The first four competencies must be in place in order for an individual to be effective in the last area – relationship management. It's our ability to manage relationships that determines the quality of our work and social lives. The emotionally intelligent person finds it easier to network than his or her emotionally unintelligent peers, easier to build effective team relationships, and easier to acknowledge and deal with constructive criticism of his or her performance.

Emotionally intelligent people recognise the positive value of constructive conflict. For more on this, head over to IDEA 32, *Hegel don't bother me.*

Try another idea...

Our ability or inability to manage relationships effectively drives much of our lives. In an organisational context, for example, leaders need the ability in order to inspire organisations to greatness, and salespeople need it to build strong and profitable customer relationships. In our personal lives, it shapes how we deal with friends and family. This can be particularly challenging. Many of us find it relatively easy to be emotionally intelligent when we're at work, but lose our tempers all to easily with those who are close to us – parents, spouses and children.

'You're not paranoid – you're the opposite of paranoid. You suffer from the insane delusion that people actually like you.'
WOODY ALLEN in *Deconstructing Harry*

Defining idea...

WHAT DOES THIS ALL MEAN IN PRACTICE?

Well, what is doesn't mean is merely 'being nice'. In fact, often being emotionally intelligent can demand confronting others – and sometimes even ourselves – with an uncomfortable but consequential truth they've been avoiding.

Likewise, emotional intelligence does not mean giving free rein to feelings – 'letting it all hang out'. Rather, it means managing feelings so that they are expressed appropriately and effectively, enabling people to work together smoothly toward their common goals.

By the way, contrary to what many people assume, women are not 'smarter' than men when it comes to emotional intelligence, nor are men superior to women. Each of us has a personal profile of strengths and weaknesses.

SO CAN WE IMPROVE OUR LEVEL OF EMOTIONAL INTELLIGENCE?

Yes, but we need to be prepared to confront problems constructively as they arise. Running away from or just ignoring problems is not emotionally intelligent; neither is losing your temper and having a rant. We can only improve our emotional intelligence by practice and by being prepared to accept feedback from others about how we are doing.

Defining idea...

'*He who digs a hole for another may fall in it himself.*'
Russian proverb

Q **When I talked with colleagues about emotional intelligence, they seemed to take the view that it was more or less fixed at birth. Were they right?**

How did it go?

A *Absolutely not. Our level of emotional intelligence is not fixed genetically, nor does it develop only in early childhood. Unlike IQ, which changes little after our teen years, emotional intelligence continues to develop as we go through life and learn from our experiences. Studies that have tracked people's level of emotional intelligence through the years show that people get better and better in these capabilities as they grow more adept at handling their own emotions and impulses, at motivating themselves, and at honing their empathy and social adeptness.*

Q **Isn't there an old-fashioned word for emotional intelligence: maturity?**

A *In some ways, yes – emotional intelligence is just another word for maturity. The concept of emotional intelligence does not necessarily invent new models of behaviour. What it serves to do is to remind us that we humans have an emotional as well as a rational base for our actions. When we are at work, we have historically emphasised the rational and buried the emotional. In many ways, the emotional intelligence movement is about redressing the balance and acknowledging the role that our emotional side plays.*

28

Caught in a decision trap

How do you know whether you're making a good decision or not? Here's a checklist for ensuring that you don't sell yourself a mental pup.

Negotiating the best path through the challenges that life holds for us often involves a mixture of those things we should positively aim to do and those things that we should definitely avoid.

The same is true of making a good decision. There are ways of making our minds up that are widely accepted as good practice and there are traps to be avoided.

Writing in *Harvard Business Review*, John S. Hammond, Ralph L. Keeney and Howard Raiffa identified eight psychological traps that are particularly likely to affect the way we make decisions:

The anchoring trap: this leads us to give disproportionate weight to the first information we receive. Somebody tells you that a new member of staff is untrustworthy; that tends to shape how you view and deal with them.

Here's an idea for you... **Spend a few moments reflecting on some of the bad decisions you've made. Are there any decision-making traps that you are particularly prone to? If so, how can you correct or compensate for that tendency in the future?**

The status-quo trap: this describes the temptation to stick with the current situation because it is familiar and known – even when better alternatives exist. It manifests itself as an overly cautious approach to changing the formula. Whenever you hear the plaintive cry 'but we've always done it that way', chances are that the speaker is fully enmeshed in the status-quo trap.

The sunk-cost trap: this leads us to carry on perpetuating the mistakes of the past. This 'I've started so I'll finish' mentality comes over as a stubborn adherence to a path of action despite mounting evidence that it's not a sensible way to proceed (remember the UK's poll tax débâcle, anyone, or the Vietnam War?).

The confirming-evidence trap: this trap leads us to seek out information supporting an existing predilection and to discount opposing information. Think of somebody famous you don't particularly like: do you experience a certain *Schadenfreude* when they get unfavourable coverage in the press or on TV?

The framing trap: this comes about when we mis-state a problem from the very start, undermining the entire decision-making process. To take a fictional example, if the government decides that public resistance to identity cards is due to concerns about cost when the reality is that the impact of their introduction on civil liberties is the real issue, then a host of ministers going on a PR offensive to announce a cap on cost completely misses the point.

The overconfidence trap: this can make us overestimate the accuracy of our forecasts. My publishers – somewhat unkindly, I feel – have suggested that my estimates of when they can expect to receive finished manuscripts fall squarely into this category.

The prudence trap: this trap leads us to be overcautious when we make estimates about uncertain events. This often stems from failing to understand the true probability of there being a bad outcome. Examples of the prudence trap are people deciding not to go on holiday to Europe because of 'all that terrorism' or to Sri Lanka because of concerns about 'another tsunami'.

The recallability trap: we fall into this trap when we give undue weight to recent, dramatic events. There are those who believe that the US response to 9/11 was a prime example. A lighter example is the tendency of some tennis fans to assume that one or two good performances by a British player means that they will be a shoo-in for the title next year.

The best way for us to avoid falling headlong into any of these traps is awareness – forewarned is forearmed. This involves our being prepared to question whether the assumptions on which a decision is based still hold good. In other words, how do we know that a piece of evidence on which we are basing our decision is still true?

Not making bad decisions is a good start, but why not take a more positive approach by reading IDEA 22, *Make the best decision you can*?

Try another idea...

'**When you have to make a choice and don't make it, that is in itself a choice.**'
WILLIAM JAMES

Defining idea...

We also need to be astute enough to recognise that there is a distinction between smart choices and good consequences. Sometimes we can make the right decision but it just doesn't turn out well for us. Equally, we can make a bad, poorly formed decision which luckily turns out well.

How did it go?

Q   When I think about it, I've made many bad decisions in my time, but aren't they just a by-product of the fact that we all have to make lots of decisions these days?

A   *To a degree, yes. What tends to happen when we have lots of decisions to make is that we get into habitual patterns of thinking and acting. What this can mean is that we are in danger of falling into the same 'bad decision trap' time and time again. By making ourselves aware of these traps, at least we give ourselves a fighting chance of spotting those that we are prone to falling into.*

Q   How can I avoid falling into these decision-making traps in the future?

A   *When we actually make a decision, it's often because we have convinced ourselves that there is a clinching argument in favour of that particular decision. The more we can articulate what the clinching argument actually is, the easier it is for us to test that argument against the known traps.*

29

Technology: be a leader, not a laggard

Technology can make us functionally more creative and intelligent. This is not a recommendation to go out and buy every latest gizmo, just an observation that we ignore the best technology at our intellectual peril.

How do we manage if we want to make intelligent use of technology but we don't necessarily want to slavishly follow every fad and technological cul-de-sac?

Enter Geoffrey Moore with his most famous model – the Technology Adoption Life Cycle. There are, according to Moore, five different categories that technology adopters can belong to, namely Innovators, Early Adopters, Early Majority, Late Majority and Laggards.

He sums them up as follows:

Innovators: these are technology enthusiasts who pursue new products aggressively. They sometimes seek them out even before they have been launched.

Here's an idea for you...

Compile a list of your technology-related possessions. Include everything, from the latest gizmo to those old vinyl albums in the loft. When you've done that, assign one of these three categories to each item: 'Need to upgrade', 'Fine as it is' and 'Past its sell-by date'. Sell off items in category 3 to help fund the purchase of those things that you need to upgrade.

This is because technology is a central interest in their lives. There are not very many innovators around – maybe 3–5 per cent of us at most – but winning them over at the outset reassures the other players in the marketplace that the product does in fact work.

Early Adopters: these are the visionaries who, like innovators, buy into new product concepts very early in their life cycle but, unlike innovators, they are not technologists. Rather, they are people who find it easy to imagine, understand and appreciate the benefits of a new technology, and to relate these potential benefits to their other concerns. Whenever they find a strong match, early adopters are willing to base their buying decisions upon it.

Early Majority: these are pragmatists who share some of the early adopters' ability to relate to technology, but ultimately are driven by a strong sense of practicality. They know that many of these new inventions end up as passing fads, so they are content to wait and see how other people are making out before they buy in themselves. Roughly one-third of us fall into this category.

Late Majority: these are the people who wait until something has become an established standard, and even then want to see lots of support before they buy, typically from large, well-established companies. Like the early majority, this group comprises about one-third of the total buying population.

Laggards: as the name suggests, these are the sceptics who simply don't want anything to do with new technology, for any of a variety of reasons, some personal and some economic. The only time they ever buy a technological product is when it is buried so deep inside another product – the way, say, that a microprocessor is designed into the braking system of a new car – that they don't even know it is there.

These days, technological advances and innovation are closely intertwined. So have a look at IDEA 24, *Innovate*.

Try another idea...

We all have to think about where we want to position ourselves relative to new technology. While there is a certain romantic appeal to living Henry Thoreau-like in a log cabin in the wilds thinking deep thoughts and blissfully free of modern technology, the plain truth is that being a Laggard is not a viable option for all but a technophobic handful.

Being one of Moore's Innovators might seem to be the group that a state-of-the-art thinker would want to be a part of. Group members are assured of a sneak preview of what is to come technologically and can get their mitts on and become accustomed to new technologies well before the hoi polloi. However, Innovators do pay premium prices for new technologies, many of which won't take off, so must display a natural and unforced enthusiasm for technology.

'Multimedia? As far as I'm concerned, it's reading with the radio on.'
RORY BREMNER, British comedian

Defining idea...

Feel free to disagree, but I suspect that pragmatic brain-upgraders would want to see the dust settle a little before deciding whether new innovations will help them to function more effectively in a knowledge economy. They wouldn't normally want to hold back as long as the Late Majority does, being thought leaders by nature rather than thought followers. So it's a toss up between being an Early Adopter or a member of the Early Majority. Both groups harness the benefits of new technologies sooner rather than later.

How did it go?

Q   I'm a real fan of new technology and can readily see the benefits. Are there any drawbacks I should be aware of?

A   *There are, of course, surveillance and privacy issues. Uninvited people, for example, can peruse your emails, lift your credit card details and be aware of your internet browsing habits. There are those who think that mobile phones are just electronic tagging by another name. On balance, technology has been a force for good, but we shouldn't ignore the downsides.*

Q   So is there an optimal position to take relative to technology?

A   *Where you choose to position yourself may well depend on the extent to which technology is a core element in your home and working lives – if it doesn't play a big role, then the argument for getting into new waves of technology ahead of your peers isn't strong. You may also find that your position changes from technology to technology. Just because, for example, you decide that having a mobile phone is an obvious boon to your lifestyle, it doesn't mean that you necessarily need to buy an iPod.*

30

Questions, questions

**The key to quality thinking is asking quality questions.
If you fancy giving yourself a mental stretch by tackling
some testing questions, here are some real doozies.**

Unless you're a politician or a criminal (or
possibly both), good incisive questions are to be
absolutely cherished. Answered honestly, they can
propel our thinking in new directions, generating
fresh insights and understanding on the way.

A good question unlocks or clarifies our current thinking. Although we can answer
almost any question – no matter how brilliantly formed – with banal platitudes if we
so wish, a good question has the potential to shake us out of any mental complacency.

The following is a list of questions I have found over the years to be productive. I've
voiced them in the first person so that you can ask them initially of yourself, but
they work equally in the second person, asked of others.

The questions are in no particular sequence. Nor would I recommend that you
tackle them all in one go. Cast your eyes over the list and see what's catches your
interest. OK then? The clock starts...now.

What do I want to achieve with my life?

What should I want?

What matters to me at this time in my life?

Why do I want what I want?

Does it really matter?

Who am I living my life for?

Here's an idea for you...

Sometimes when people are answering questions their initial response doesn't go far or deep enough. In case this happens, prepare some supplementary questions to keep to hand. Asking 'Can you be more specific?' or 'Do you have anything else to say on this subject?' can help to keep the exploration of the question going in a productive manner.

What don't I know?

What do I not question about myself?

What can I learn from this?

What are my plans for the next year?

What support do I need in order to...? Who can help me?

How ambitious am I these days?

Am I still learning and growing?

What needs my attention today/this week/this month/this year?

If I died tomorrow, what would be missing from my obituary that I would like to see there? What can I do about it?

What am I afraid of losing?

What am I afraid of gaining?

What would I like to overhear people saying about me?

What would I not like to hear said about me?

Why is my best friend my best friend?

Would winning the lottery be a blessing or a curse?

What would I do if I knew I couldn't fail?

Is that all there is to this?

How do I know this to be true?

In what way am I causing or reinforcing this behaviour?

If I had a year to live, what would I do with the time?

How do I feel when I get up in the morning?

When have I felt most alive?

Does my reputation work for or against me?

Sometimes we don't need to ask questions, but just give people space to talk. See IDEA 21, *It's good to talk*.

Try another idea...

What would I like to be able to do in one year's time that I can't currently do? Or five years from now? Ten years? Twenty-five years? Fifty years? One hundred years? (You never know)

What action can I take rather than worrying?

What am I prepared to give up in order to...?

What's the best outcome in this situation? And the worst?

What could affect my plans?

'I refuse to answer that question on the grounds that I don't know the answer.'
DOUGLAS ADAMS

Defining idea...

135

What do I need to do to make sure that I get what I want?

What's the best thing I've done in the last year and why?

What do I need to find out before I go any further?

What aspects of my life do I enjoy the most? And the least?

Why not?

What could other people learn from me?

So how did you get on? Of course, you asking yourself those questions might feel like a slightly stilted experience. For that reason, it can be worthwhile to get somebody else to put the questions to you. For one thing, that gets you to speak your answers aloud, and that in itself can be quite instructive. Sometimes it's only when we hear ourselves say something out loud that we realise how true it is for us (or occasionally how wrong we are!).

Q **Good grief! All this self-reflection. Wasn't the mighty Elvis right when he commended 'a little less conversation, a little more action'?**

How did it go?

A *Of course, there is always a balance to be struck between thinking and action. A book like this is inevitably going to focus more on thinking models and processes, and as a result commend a more considered approach to making decisions and acting on them. Was it not the same Elvis who noted that 'wise men say only fools rush in'?*

Q **Eschewing the opportunity to trade more Elvis lines, can you highlight any of the questions that you believe to be particularly useful and productive?**

A *They all have their place, naturally. The three questions that I think have particular value are:*

How do I know this to be true? (A great question for testing assumptions.)

What do I want to accomplish with my life? (In many ways, the biggest question of all.)

What can I learn from this? (All progress – collective and personal – depends on our ability to draw conclusions from our experience.)

31

Excel is not just a spreadsheet

What does it take to excel at something? Turns out it's a mixture of vision, commitment, hard graft and a sprinkling of talent.

My guess is that your goal in life isn't just to be average or OK or not bad in everything you do. Go on, admit it. You want to be stonkingly good at something.

Personal mastery begins with a vision of what you want to achieve with your life. That's also where the problems start. Most of us rub along with little sense of real vision. We might have a few goals and objectives, but these are not visions. It's perfectly reasonable to want to retire, for example, but it's hardly inspiring. Often our goals are more about what we don't want than what we do. We might say that we want a better job, but actually our primary desire is to be rid of our current job.

Having a personal vision is about a desire to apply a sense of purpose to something that is really meaningful to us. For some people, a personal vision has quasi-religious or mystical overtones because it answers the question: Why am I here? For others, it's an entirely earthbound drive to excel that is underpinned by the sense that life

139

Here's an idea for you... **Don't be the world's best kept secret. Once you know in which area(s) you wish to attain personal mastery, tell other people what you aspire to. The more we become known for being something, the more likely it is that others at different places on the same journey will consciously seek us out.**

is not a dress rehearsal. Wherever the drive comes from, it's about wanting something passionately.

Let's be clear, though – wanting something and making it happen are different things. I might enjoy rowing and have a fancy to become a future Olympic champion. But am I prepared to commit to the regime necessary to get anywhere near the necessary level of excellence?

Personal mastery involves taking personal responsibility for making something happen. It is a journey that starts when we come to realise that we are master of our own destiny.

Writer and consultant Peter Senge writes about personal mastery in his book *The Fifth Discipline*, where he describes it as follows:

'Personal mastery goes beyond competence and skills, though it is grounded in competence and skills. It goes beyond spiritual unfolding or opening, although it requires spiritual growth. It means approaching one's life as a creative work, living life from a creative as opposed to a reactive viewpoint...People with high levels of personal mastery are continually expanding their ability to create the results in life they truly seek.'

When we talk about personal mastery, some people have a problem with the language used, which often seems to be drawn from those slightly smug self-help texts. All this talk of 'life purpose', 'spiritual growth' and 'being on a journey' is not necessarily everyone's cup of tea. It's worth emphasising that somebody who has attained a level of personal mastery over their chosen field is just as likely to be a salt-of-the-earth pragmatist as a sandal-wearing mystic.

Pop along to IDEA 46, *Become a core competent*, for a look at how to build up your knowledge base.

Try another idea...

Once we have a vision of what we want to become, what separates the achievers from the dreamers is a willingness to commit to the pursuit of the vision. A friend of mine once told me about a fortune cookie motto she came across: You can achieve whatever is most important to you in the world as long as you are prepared to forgo whatever is second most important. The choice may not be absolutely that stark – it is possible to have your cake and eat at least some of it – but personal mastery does require a certain single-mindedness.

There's a Zen saying: After enlightenment, the laundry. Personal mastery too is a combination of the glory days and the hard yards. But once you commit energy and resources to becoming whatever it is you want to be, you will find that you become automatically more alert to opportunities to develop your talent.

You may have had that experience where you buy a new car and all of a sudden the roads are awash with people driving your car (not your actual car – that would be a little inconvenient). When we focus in on something, we tend to go out and discover

'*Personal mastery teaches us to choose. Choosing is a courageous act: picking the results and actions which you will make into your destiny.*'
PETER SENGE

Defining idea...

people, events, courses, opportunities and so on that are highly relevant to our journey. Those other cars were always there – you just hadn't noticed them before.

How did it go?

Q   **I find this personal mastery stuff a bit wearisome. What's so wrong with being happy to be OK or average at something?**

A   *Regardless of the moral or philosophical angle, looking to make the most of what you have is a good life strategy because it gives you your best chance of long-term participation in the economic marketplace. These days, being OK at what you do isn't good enough. Perhaps it was sufficient when jobs were for life, and our lives changed incrementally. Nowadays, aiming for adequacy is a recipe for the scrapheap.*

Q   **Is personal mastery all about doing one thing very, very well, then?**

A   *Only partly. Really, it's more of a life philosophy: it's a belief that we should aspire to put a bit of heart and commitment into everything we do with our lives.*

32

Hegel don't bother me

Conflict can be good for us (as long as it's resolved quickly) and it can lead to better quality solutions to our problems. Unresolved conflict is the killer.

Back in prehistoric times, when our ancestors were preoccupied with survival rather than the daily Sudoku puzzle, they dealt with physical threat by either facing squarely up to it or by disappearing sharpish from the danger spot.

Fight or flight? Choosing the right option was literally a matter of life or death.

This is not just a matter of historical interest. Many psychologists believe that the human race is still hardwired to respond to danger in one of these two ways.

Nowadays, the source of the threat is more likely to be our boss than a hairy mammoth (not always a lot of difference between the two, I accept), and the nature of the threat is more likely to be mental rather than physical. But whether it's a fist heading in our direction or a 'dangerous' idea, we are still likely to encounter biochemical changes in our body or our brain that our Neolithic ancestors would recognise.

Here's an idea for you... **When you next find yourself having a disagreement, try summarising what the other person is saying from time to time. This will help to clarify the issue and demonstrates that you are listening and trying to understand, and suggests that you are genuinely keen to find a resolution.**

The trouble is that the world has moved on, and effective problem solving in the twenty-first century requires a more sophisticated set of options. It was Georg Wilhelm Friedrich Hegel, the nineteenth-century German philosopher, who came up with the notion of a 'synthesis of opposites', the idea that a thesis could be juxtaposed with its opposite number (or antithesis) to generate synthesis, a new configuration that both includes and rises above the foundational elements. This phenomenon is known as a 'Hegelian dialectic'.

If we apply the Hegelian dialectic to the thesis of 'fight' versus the antithesis of 'flight', it is possible to achieve a synthesis – let's call it 'confront and problem solve'.

It's not a common approach – research shows that European organisations manage conflict by smoothing over and avoiding it 50 per cent of the time, aggressively confronting it 30 per cent of the time and constructively confronting it only 20 per cent of the time. But look beyond the Western mindset and we find that the Japanese, for example, have achieved much of their industrial success over the years by embracing the principle of synthesis.

Richard Pascale, writer, consultant and a member of the Stanford faculty for over twenty years, is a firm advocate of the need to move beyond thinking in absolute categories (like right or wrong and black or white), to thinking that can reconcile opposites. Pascale calls this transition the move from 'either/or' to 'both/and'.

So how can we harness constructive conflict in practice?

A *Harvard Business Review* article by Kathleen Eisenhardt, Jean Kahwajy and L.J. Bourgeois III suggests five ways to achieve this in a work context:

Conflict can be reduced sometimes by having the right environment. More on this in IDEA 7, *Thinks ain't what they used to be.*

Try another idea...

1. Assemble a team with diverse ages, backgrounds and industry experience.
2. Meet frequently to build familiarity and mutual confidence.
3. Encourage team members to assume roles outside of their obvious functional responsibilities, and so discourage 'turf war' thinking.
4. Apply multiple perspectives – role playing, putting yourself in your competitor's shoes, etc. This can enable a fresh view of the problem.
5. Actively and overtly manage conflict. Ensure that consensus is real and not just an indication of disengagement.

'Honest disagreement is often a good sign of progress.'
MOHANDAS GANDHI

Defining idea...

Whether we are at work or at home, there are four key elements involved in handling conflict well:

1. Develop a commonly agreed goal. Once all parties have agreed what the overall objective is, it becomes a lot easier to frame decisions as collaborations.
2. As far as possible, depersonalise the conversation. If the discussion becomes characterised in terms of doing something Linda's way or Barbara's way, things can rapidly descend into a battle of personalities. So aim to debate on the basis of facts.

'I don't want yes men around me. I want everyone to tell the truth, even if it costs them their jobs.'
SAM GOLDWYN

Defining idea...

3. Develop multiple alternatives. Research shows that the more choices there are on offer, the less likely unconstructive argument is to break out.
4. Keep a sense of humour. Humour has a powerful positive effect on people's moods. When the discussion is kept playful and light, people listen more and are generally less defensive.

How did it go?

Q **I've tried to disagree constructively with my boss but it's clear that she doesn't like having her opinion questioned. How does constructive conflict work when that's the case?**

A *It doesn't! It's very important to keep a balanced power structure in the process of resolving conflict. If somebody is going to play the 'I'm the friggin' boss and what I say goes' card at the drop of a hat, other people are unlikely to engage in the process. Sam Goldwyn, the movie mogul, summed up this unconstructive managerial outlook brilliantly when he said: 'When I want your opinion I will give it to you.'*

Q **OK, my boss has had a change of heart and is willing to give constructive conflict a go. How can he be certain that he won't go down in the estimation of his staff by appearing weak?**

A *Results are what count. Your boss needs to explain that he has come to realise that many heads come up with a better quality solution than just one head. He also needs to demonstrate that the input of his team makes a genuine difference to the decisions arrived at. When he disagrees with his team, he should be able to explain why. And he'll need to give genuine, substantive reasons – 'because I'm in charge' just won't pass muster.*

33
Should I share or should I hoard?

It's the twenty-first-century knowledge worker's dilemma – whether to share their personal intellectual capital with others or to guard it jealously.

You may have heard that Woody Allen line: 90 per cent of success at work is about turning up.

Perhaps that was true once, but these days most of us know that if we don't 'add value' where we work then we're out.

According to a study led by Adrian Patch, a research psychologist at Birkbeck College in London, some of us knowledge workers have responded to the end of the job-for-life culture by becoming 'professional parasites', hoarding our expertise in the fear that sharing knowledge makes us more dispensable.

Patch's study uncovered tensions between companies who have put in computer infrastructures to enable the sharing of knowledge and information, and their employees who are not willing to do so. Patch reported that one in five workers thought it was not in his or her interest to share knowledge at work, costing business billions of pounds a year in missed business opportunities, inefficient systems and training.

Here's an idea for you... **When it comes to assessing your value in the market place, try thinking of yourself as a brand. To help you define your brand, ask yourself: What do I want to be known for? Now what can you do over the next twelve months to add value to your brand?**

Those who feel threatened or unappreciated at work guard their niche knowledge jealously, making effective teamwork – which depends on the open exchange of information – virtually impossible. Companies who encourage employees to manage their own careers, but who at the same time create dissatisfaction by failing to fulfil their promises, risk losing important knowledge that is often a key part of the company's value.

So what are we knowledge workers to do for the best? We know that knowledge confers tremendous power on those who possess it. In the short term, sharing our expertise makes us personally less valuable to the organisation and that potentially puts us in the frame to be 'let go' by employers if costs ever need cutting.

On the other hand, our knowledge is not like gold anymore – it's not something whose value will rise and therefore something to be preserved and hoarded. No, these days our knowledge is more like milk: it has a short shelf-life and so needs to be used quickly. For the knowledge worker who wants to play a more long-term game, the key question becomes this: 'How can I best build on my current know-how as well as acquire the knowledge I'll need in order to be relevant to employers in the years to come?'

The conclusion that more and more knowledge workers are coming to is that it is not a good strategy to continue ploughing a solo furrow, neither giving their knowledge away nor benefiting from the expertise of their colleagues. They've twigged that what they give is what they get, and so the best long-term strategy is to act collaboratively and to forge positive links with other colleagues. In a nutshell, the best survival strategy for a knowledge worker is to become a fully fledged team player.

If you want to be a sharer not a hoarder, you'll need to get out and meet a few people. There's more on networking at IDEA 10, *Why use your own brain when you can borrow other people's?*

Try another idea...

When teams learn together, not only can there be good results for the organisation, but also individuals grow and learn more rapidly, as well as feeling that they belong to something meaningful. Peter Senge, populariser of the learning organisation concept, puts it like this:

'When you ask people about what it is like being part of a great team, what is most striking is the meaningfulness of the experience. People talk about being part of something larger than themselves, of being connected, of being generative. It become quite clear that, for many, their experiences as part of truly great teams stand out as singular periods of life lived to the fullest. Some spend the rest of their lives looking for ways to recapture that spirit.'

For most of us in organisations, success often depends on surrounding yourself with the very best people. Working collaboratively is far more likely to deliver good results and improve our personal capabilities than working competitively. Perhaps we are coming to recognise ain important truth: that moving from dependence to independence is a sign of growing up, but that moving from independence to interdependence is a sign of maturity.

'Intellectual property has the shelf-life of a banana.'
BILL GATES

Defining idea...

How did it go?

Q   **I've got a problem with a knowledge hoarder in my team. How can I convince him that it's better to be a sharer?**

A   *People who hoard do so because they consider it logical and natural to do so. They need to understand that they personally will benefit by sharing their knowledge and that they don't jeopardise their position by doing so. Personal benefits are that they are likely to be given information in return, which increases their knowledge basis and hence their market value. Companies are much more likely to invest in training people who will share their knowledge.*

Q   **So what can I do to make it more natural for my whole team to share their knowledge and expertise?**

A   *Build knowledge sharing into the day-to-day practices of your team. For example, when somebody goes on a training course, automatically build in a slot at the next team meeting for them to share the key points of learning. At pay review time, reward those who share more than those who hoard. Encourage your team members to meet up with other experts in their field. If people persistently prove reluctant to share their knowledge, divert resources away from them and in the direction of those who do share.*

150

34

Trust me – I'm a salesman

Here's an insight into how marketing and sales people try to influence our behaviour. Interestingly, we could deploy most of their influencing techniques ourselves if we wished.

Did you know that the average UK citizen is exposed to over 3,000 advertising messages every day?

While most of us imagine that we are immune to the charms of the advertising industry, people trying to sell us stuff are becoming every more sophisticated in their approach.

Robert B. Cialdini, a professor of psychology at Arizona State University, is best known for his popular book on persuasion and marketing, *Influence: the Psychology of Persuasion*. As part of his research for writing the book, he spent three years 'undercover', applying for jobs and training at used car dealerships, fund-raising organisations, telemarketing companies and so on, observing real-life situations of persuasion.

Through his research, Cialdini was able to identify six 'weapons of influence' that canny marketing and sales professionals deploy in order to influence our behaviour as consumers. On the principle that to be forewarned is to be forearmed, let's have a look at these six weapons:

Here's an idea for you... **If you're trying to persuade somebody to do something, don't invent pretend relatives who live in their home town or who went to the same university. Instead, go down the ethical track and find something that you genuinely have in common with the person. It's not that difficult to find a shared experience – a bar or a restaurant you've both been to, a movie you've both seen, your response to a recent news item. Once you've found this common link, it will help your persuasive cause.**

Reciprocation

According to sociologists and anthropologists, this is one of the most basic 'rules' of human culture. Put simply, we tend to feel obligated to return a favour. This is why one favorite sales tactic is to give us free samples before asking for a return favour.

Commitment and consistency

We like to look consistent in our words, beliefs, attitudes and deeds. Once we agree to make a commitment toward a goal or idea, we are likely to honour that commitment. Even if an incentive is removed after we have already agreed terms, we will often continue to honour the agreement. So a car salesman can suddenly raise the price at the last moment without losing the sale because we have already decided to buy.

Social proof

People will do things that they see other people are doing. So if you want a 6-year-old to do something, let him or her discover another 6-year-old doing it.

Liking

People prefer to say yes to individuals they know and like. Physical attractiveness seems to create a 'halo' effect that extends to our perception of the other person's talent, kindness, intelligence and so on. As a result, attractive people are often highly persuasive in terms of getting what they request and in changing others' attitudes. The degree of similarity also influences liking. We like people who are like us, and are more willing to say yes to their requests. When a salesperson asks you where you live and then claims to have an aunt who lives there, there's a fighting chance that they are playing the similarity card.

For a more classical view of the art of persuasion, have a look at IDEA 20, *What did the Greeks ever do for us?*

Try another idea...

Authority

There's a strong tendency in our society to comply with the requests of an authority. When reacting to authority, we tend to respond as much to symbols of authority – titles, clothing, etc. – as to its substance. This explains why we can find it difficult to ignore the head waiter's recommendations for what's good on the menu.

'Ridicule is the best test of truth. The more we can puncture an argument, the less truthful it is.'
ROBERT CIALDINI, influence expert

Defining idea...

Scarcity

According to the scarcity principle, people assign more value to opportunities when they are less available. The use of this principle for profit can be seen in techniques such as the 'limited edition' and 'offer must end on Saturday' tactics, where the salesperson tries to convince us that access to what they are offering is restricted by amount or time. We also value

scarce items more when we have to compete with others for them. This explains why we might pay over the odds for an item being auctioned on eBay.

You should find it helpful to understand how these weapons of choice are deployed by those who are trying to influence our behaviour and our purchasing habits. Of course, now that we know about this stuff, there's nothing to stop us from using these techniques ourselves!

How did it go?

Q I've tried some of these techniques and alarmingly they seem to work! Is it really just a matter of pressing the right levers and people will respond the way you want them to?

A *Cialdini's research does suggest that the methods he has identified will consistently get good results. There will always be exceptions of course, but, by and large, the levers work.*

Q If these methods are so effective, why don't more people know about them?

A *Most of Cialdini's findings are already familiar to a degree. After all, he actually observed these methods in use in a wide range of settings – he didn't invent them. What he did achieve, though, was the codification of methods that were used sporadically into an integrated and coherent system. Why his findings aren't better known is a bit of a mystery – though he is an academic by training, so perhaps he didn't set out to make his model universally known.*

35

From Masterchef to Mastermind – eat your way to genius

Here's some food for thought: a look at the latest research into how the way we eat affects the way we think.

Two thousand years ago, Roman poet Juvenal gave the world the phrase 'mens sana in corpore sano', which translates as 'a healthy mind in a healthy body'.

If you have ever tried to eat eighteen doughnuts, drink six pints and then tackle a particularly fiendish Sudoku puzzle (it was for a bet, alright?), then you will recognise the wisdom in Juvenal's words. There is a distinct correlation between the quality of our diet and the quality of our thinking.

Although you might not think so from the vast array of diet books stuffing up the market, the basics of healthy eating and drinking are actually very simple. There are seven simple rules:

Here's an idea for you...

Don't rely on supplements as a route to rude health. Although it's tempting to pop a few pills as a shortcut to getting the nutrients we need, most nutritionists recommend a balanced diet. This is because our bodies absorb nutrients from the food we eat much more efficiently than from a supplement. This is partly because the nutrients in our system work together to enhance absorption. Also, even a single food like milk can contain many different nutrients.

Over half of your diet should be made up of complex carbohydrates. These are foods such as bread, cereals, rice and pasta. If you can, try to eat the wholewheat and wholemeal varieties, because these are high in fibre and are nearer to food in its natural state. Oat biscuits, oatcakes, flapjacks and fruit (apart from starchy fruits like bananas) are very good for increasing energy levels and improving concentration because they provide a steady and extended release of energy.

Eat less fat. In general you should try to ensure that fat makes up no more than 30 per cent of your diet, especially those nasty saturated animal fats. If you are looking to lose some weight, you should try to decrease your fat intake to no more than 20 per cent.

Eat less sugar. Sugar is just empty calories and has no nutritional value whatsoever. Avoid eating sweets when you are attending a meeting or training session; sweets have a high sugar content that gets the blood glucose rocketing sky high – the so-called sugar hit. The trouble is that your blood glucose levels crash quickly and spectacularly from this high, leaving you feeling lethargic and having difficulty in concentrating.

Eat more fruit and vegetables. Aim for at least five portions a day.

Forget the regulation meat and two veg. Your everyday norm for main meals should be bread, potatoes, rice or pasta with plenty of vegetables or salad, though you can include a little lean meat or fish if you wish.

Steer clear of ready-prepared meals as far as possible. They typically contain more of the bad stuff (sugar, fat, etc.) and less of the good stuff than their unprocessed equivalents.

Drink plenty of water, and keep your weekly alcohol intake under control. In other words, don't drink more than a few drinks in one sitting, have at least two alcohol-free days a week and don't drink more than the recommended weekly units.

Stick to these principles and you shouldn't go far wrong.

By the way, be a bit wary of coffee because it has a mixed track record. Physiologically, the caffeine in coffee makes us feel alert, and pumps adrenaline to give us energy. Caffeine also increases dopamine, which in turn activates the pleasure in parts of the brain. Experiments carried out at Cardiff University to examine the effects of coffee on performance and alertness during the day and at night showed that caffeinated coffee had a beneficial effect on alertness and improved performance on a variety of tasks in both day and night sessions.

Research conducted in the Netherlands found that coffee had a positive impact on selective attention and speed of information processing. It also found some evidence that caffeine in commonly consumed food

There's more on the connection between mental and physical health in IDEA 40, *Bring your body up to scratch.*

Try another idea...

'Students are getting wise to the fact that by using a good diet to aid their studying, they can boost their performance at this vital time. Word is obviously going round universities and colleges because each year sales of brainpower foods go up around this time [the lead-up to exams].'
PETER DUROSE, Produce Director at Tesco

Defining idea...

and drinks may alleviate the decline in age-related memory performance to some degree.

Less positively, caffeine is a diuretic and so causes fluid loss and therefore dehydration. This interferes with our ability to concentrate, and makes us feel lacklustre and tired. It can also affect our sleep, making it difficult for us to achieve deep sleep, which can then have a negative knock-on effect on performance the next day. Finally, for some people, the caffeine in coffee causes levels of restlessness, headaches and general irritability.

How did it go?

Q   I'm somebody who likes their pies. Does it matter if I'm a bit overweight?

A   The evidence generally suggests that being overweight is not that good for our health. In terms of a link between being overweight and brain function, there's not much firm evidence at this stage. Which means there's no evidence to suggest that the extra kilos are in any way good for our mental functioning.

Q   I like my pint of beer. Is there any harm in that?

A   In moderation, no. Heavy drinking is not good for you, of course, particularly as you're female. Recent research by a team at the University of Heidelberg has found that women are far more vulnerable to alcohol-induced brain damage than men. CT pictures of the brains of over 150 volunteers revealed that women come to more harm more quickly than their male counterparts when they drink heavily. So a sex change might be the answer; on the other hand, you could just cut down a bit.

36

Memories are made of this

How the memory works, and what you can do to improve yours.

The last thirty years have seen tremendous advances in our understanding of how the brain works. Scientists can pinpoint with increasing confidence which parts of the brain perform which specific function.

However, as far as memory improvement is concerned, there's not a lot of new advice out there. There is some interesting research emerging from America (where else?) into the use of pharmaceutical pick-me-ups called ampakines as a tool for boosting mental performance, but it's still early days in the clinical trial process.

When it comes to recalling information more readily, the basic techniques for enabling this have not changed substantially for decades. Back in 1956, psychologist George A. Miller published a paper that helped to spark the cognitive revolution. The paper was called 'The magical number seven, plus or minus two: some limits on our capacity for processing information'. Miller's research revealed that the average human can hold only about seven items in mind at any one time. Some can hold only five items while others can comfortably manage up to nine.

On the basis that practice makes perfect, simply repeating the information is a good memory aid. Remember the children's game 'I'm going on a picnic and I'm bringing...' As each new object is added, the old objects are repeated. People can often remember a large number of objects this way. When remembering a list of things, you might try a similar concept, maybe 'I'm going to a very important meeting and I need to...'

This natural limitation on our capacity to remember has been with us for centuries and it helps to explain why we have needed to develop methods and techniques to help us extend our capacity to remember information.

The word 'mnemonics' originally meant the study and development of systems for improving the memory. Over time, the word has come to be commonly used to describe the systems themselves. Here are some examples of mnemonics:

Spelling mnemonics: these help us remember how to spell tricky words by creating memorable sentences with words whose first letters 'spell out' the word in question. For example, RHYTHM: Rhythm Helps Your Two Hips Move.

Numeric mnemonics: these help us to remember numbers via sentences whose words have the number of letters corresponding to the number itself. Example: a sentence to help us remember that the value of pi = 3.141592 might be 'How I wish I could calculate pi.'

Acrostics: this entails using the first letter of each word you are trying to remember to make a sentence. For example, My Dear Aunt Sally would help us recall the mathematical order of operations – Multiply and Divide before you Add and Subtract.

Rhyming mnemonics: e.g. 'Thirty days hath September, April, June and November.'

For more on keeping your brain in tip-top nick, have a look at **IDEA 52**, *Maintain your brain*.

Try another idea...

Chunking: a method for remembering long numbers by breaking them down. So 04711998 might break down to 04 71 19 98. If there are combinations of numbers which are meaningful to you, so much the better. You might want to recast the number as 04 71 (the month and year I was born) and 1998 (the year our first child was born).

Number/rhyme: typically used for remembering up to ten items. For the numbers one to ten, you first come up with a rhyming word. Common rhymes are One: Bun, Two: Shoe, Three: Tree. You then assign the word you want to remember to a number. So you might assign the word 'burglar' to the number one. You then come up with a visual image associating 'burglar' with your rhyming word for one, namely 'bun'. (Hope you're keeping up with this.) The more memorable the image the better. You end up with a set of images which feature the word you want to remember, and because you've created a memorable association, you're more likely to recall the word.

'A memory is what is left when something happens and does not completely unhappen.'
EDWARD DE BONO

Defining idea...

Number/shape: a variation on number/rhyme, but instead of using One: Bun, you come up with a shape to represent the numbers. So the number 1 might be a pencil or a poker, 2 might be a swan. You then associate the word with the shape. So our burglar has to be associated with a poker in this case – shouldn't be too difficult to come up with a visual image for that one.

'The two offices of memory are collection and distribution.'
SAMUEL JOHNSON

Defining idea...

The story method: similar to number/rhyme, except that the images are linked together as part of a story. This makes it easier to remember the order of events and create a memorable mnemonic.

How did it go?

Q   I really struggle to remember the names of people I meet. Any tips?

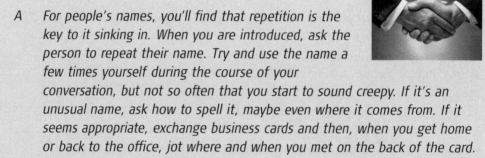

A   *For people's names, you'll find that repetition is the key to it sinking in. When you are introduced, ask the person to repeat their name. Try and use the name a few times yourself during the course of your conversation, but not so often that you start to sound creepy. If it's an unusual name, ask how to spell it, maybe even where it comes from. If it seems appropriate, exchange business cards and then, when you get home or back to the office, jot where and when you met on the back of the card.*

Q   I've not been getting much sleep recently. I feel OK but I can't help thinking that I'm not at my mental best. Is it really affecting me or is it all in my mind?

A   *No, it's not in your mind – and you are absolutely right. Skimping on sleep does awful things to your brain, reducing your ability to plan, solve problems, learn and concentrate. Your level of alertness suffers and your IQ score tumbles. Apparently, if you have been awake for 21 hours straight, your abilities are equivalent to someone who would legally be defined as drunk.*

37

Become an ace storyteller

The everyday genius is somebody who can connect with people. When it comes to convincing an audience, lose the Powerpoint slides and tell a good tale.

Cast your mind back to when you last watched a TV charity event. How did they persuade so many people on the night to part with their cash?

Of course, in reality, there were a cocktail of factors in play. But do you recall seeing anybody during the course of the evening use a Powerpoint presentation jam-packed with graphs and facts to demonstrate that making a donation is a rational and sensible act? No, the most powerful and appealing parts of the evening were the stories we heard of people who were in dire straits, but who – thanks to our past contributions – were able to recover and thrive.

The message is simple: if you want to appeal to an audience's rational side, use logic and slides; if you want to connect with an audience at a deeper, more emotional level, tell them a story.

When you tell a story, try to sound spontaneous, not as though you've told the tale hundreds of times before. To that end, don't memorise stories word for word, just go for key words and phrases. That way, you can incorporate off-the-cuff material as well.

I know a chief executive who has a reputation for being a hard-nosed pragmatist with an unwavering focus on the bottom line. His staff would be amazed to see him at weekends, when he can regularly be found watching a movie like *Carousel* and blubbing into a box of tissues. For most of us, our rational defences are so much sturdier than our emotional defences.

Storytelling is of course an ancient tradition. For as long as we have be lobbing rocks at advancing sabre-toothed tigers and surviving, we have been telling the tale afterwards. There probably isn't an adult alive who hasn't at one time been read or told a story by a parent, a grandparent, a teacher or a friend.

Given that stories have an extraordinary power to inform, educate and entertain us, it's not surprising that more and more people are turning to storytelling as a tool for consciously bringing about change in others.

In his book *The Springboard: How Storytelling Ignites Action in Knowledge-Era Organizations*, Stephen Denning, former Program Director/Knowledge Management at the World Bank, puts forward the idea that we can learn how to use storytelling to inspire others to action. He offers us these simple yet critical guidelines to help us achieve results with our storytelling:

Make your stories relevant: for a story to be effective, know as much about your audience's world as possible.

Have clear goals: occasionally, stories grow in the telling, but by and large it's easier to construct a story when you know in advance what you are trying to accomplish with it.

Use unusual examples to illustrate your point: the story has to have something unexpected happen, otherwise it's boring. 'I went to the shops and I bought some Shreddies. Then I came home. That's it.' is not likely to grip the reader.

Keep it plausible: for stories to resonate with us emotionally, we have to care about what we are hearing. If stories become too far-fetched or improbable, they lose a lot of their power to affect us.

(As far as possible) choose a story that's true: using fictitious examples to make a point weakens the impact of the story and can distract the audience.

Make the story recent: the fresher the story, the better.

Let the listeners fill in the blanks: you need to provide enough detail to communicate the point, but give the audience some space to imagine how the story could play out. The aim is to make it as easy as possible for them to draw some personal meaning from the story. The more detail the storyteller gives, the greater the risk of alienating the audience by pointing up discrepancies between the story and what's real for audience members.

> Great storytellers are great listeners – that's where many of their stories come from! For more on how to cup an ear to good effect, check out IDEA 42, *OK, repeat after me...*

Try another idea...

> 'There have been great societies that did not use the wheel, but there have been no societies that did not tell stories.'
> URSULA LE GUIN

Defining idea...

165

Naturally, the best way to improve your storytelling skills is through practice. Also, you might want to go and watch others telling stories; this can be informative in terms of both good and bad practice. So, the next time a charity event airs on TV, watch and give, but also watch and learn.

How did it go?

Q **I tried telling a story but I've got a nagging feeling I may have over-complicated things by involving half a dozen different characters. Do you think I might have over-egged it a bit?**

A *Definitely. The key to telling an effective story in a short period of time is to keep things very simple. Aim to use just a single protagonist. According to Stephen Denning: 'When you're working in a narrative form, you are trying to get the listener to live the experience of a protagonist. It's more powerful to have the listener empathise with a single individual than with hundreds. The listener is then able to live the story.'*

Q **Got that. Anything else I should bear in mind?**

A *Most stories have a simple core structure that can be boiled down to three elements – a situation, then a complication, then a resolution. The only additional element you might want to add in is 'the moral of the story'. You are presumably telling your story with some kind of intention in mind. Spend a bit of time drawing the implications of the story out so that the audience is in no doubt as to your message.*

38

What is the sound of one hand clapping?

A paradox nudges your mind away from the routine. It helps you to disengage your rational mind and to free up your intuition. Worth knowing about, then.

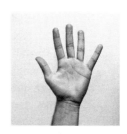

'The test of a first-rate intelligence is the ability to hold two opposed ideas in mind at the same time and still retain the ability to function.'

I wish I'd thought of that line but I cannot tell a lie – it was the *Great Gatsby* man F. Scott Fitzgerald who said it.

To a degree, Fitzgerald was running against the cultural grain in making that observation. Although embracing paradox (which I'll define here as an apparently self-contradictory or counter-intuitive statement or argument) has long been an integral part of Zen teachings, we have become accustomed in Western society to view the world in very narrow open/shut, black/white, either/or terms. But the most capable thinkers amongst us have always looked beyond either/or to both/and. Instead of seeing just polarisation, they see beyond the contradictions that many people find limiting and restrictive.

Here's an idea for you...

Paradox is part of the fabric of all our lives so we had better get used to the idea. Build up your familiarity with the notion of paradox by investing in (and reading) a book about Zen. Alternatively, put something like 'Zen quotes' into Google and see where that takes you.

Oscar Wilde is a brilliant demonstration of this. 'It is only very shallow people', he observed, 'who do not judge by appearances.' Again, 'Those who try to lead the people can only do so by following the mob.' Or, 'Man is least himself when he talks in his own person. Give him a mask, and he will tell you the truth.'

People like Wilde are able to manage the third position that emerges from balancing two opposites. As professor, consultant and author Charles Handy points out in his book, *The Age of Paradox*, 'paradox does not have to be resolved, only managed'.

Certainly if we look at the world of work, paradox is at the heart of many of the apparently contradictory messages from management gurus, academics and writers. Organisations are exhorted to stick to the knitting, decentralise, empower, direct, dream, apply common sense, be flexible and adaptive, lead the industry, benchmark, reinvent themselves, absorb best practice, delight the customer, become quality oriented, remain lean and mean, establish community, kindle the human spirit and meet the expectations of the stock market or funding body. It is no wonder that many business and community leaders take management 'fads' with a pinch of salt.

Faced with these contradictions, it's not surprising that many of us working in organisations play it safe with the result that nothing much seems to happen. Exhortations about the need for change fall on deaf ears, and the best-laid plans for change come to nothing.

There are, of course, some famous paradoxes. Take, for example, the Abilene paradox, which states the following: people can make decisions based not on what they actually want to do, but on what they think that other people want to do. As a result, everybody decides to do something that nobody really wants to do, but only what they thought that everybody else wanted to do.

Dealing with paradox can create conflict, so for a few tips on dealing with it, see IDEA 32, Hegel don't bother me.

Try another idea...

Or the Grandfather paradox: you travel back in time and kill your grandfather before he meets your grandmother. This precludes your own conception, so therefore you couldn't go back in time and kill your grandfather.

Why is it that managing paradox is so challenging for many of us? It's partly because we are unused to confronting or reconciling contradiction, and partly because many of us see paradox as a conceptual challenge rather than something which has relevance to us in our real lives.

This perception might hold some truth, but the fact is that paradox does exist in our daily lives. I often walk to my local shopping centre because it's quicker to walk that to catch a bus. We buy larger packets of cereal because they are better value only to find that we end up eating bigger portions and so any saving is lost.

The point about paradoxes is that we need to be alert to them. Ignoring them doesn't make them go away. It's only by embracing paradox that we give ourselves our best chance to reconcile them in our favour.

'A paradox, a paradox, A most ingenious paradox. Ha, ha, ha, ha, ha, ha, ha, ha, That paradox.'
Gilbert & Sullivan's *The Pirates of Penzance*

Defining idea...

How did it go?

Q I both understand and yet am confused by the idea of paradox. But tell me this: how on earth does the ability to recognise a paradox improve life for us?

A *Very good – most amusing. To answer your question, the challenge is to recognise the paradoxes and strains, and then find solutions that can integrate both sides of the dilemma. Once we are aware of these tension points, we can develop strategies for coping with them.*

Q Still a bit too conceptual for me. Could I have a practical example, please?

A This happened to me a few weeks ago. While taking a just-washed load out of the washing machine, I noticed that the clothes were damper than usual – and yet the washing machine seemed to be functioning OK. When I thought about it, the same thing had been happening for a little while. The problem continued and in fact worsened over the next few washes, so I finally decided to investigate. It turned out that a filter needed changing as it was stopping water from flowing away freely from the machine. Not a paradox to test the greatest minds, I admit, but how often do we half-notice that things 'aren't quite right' without taking any kind of action until the problem becomes explicit? The more aware we become of the existence of paradoxes in our lives, the more they can serve as an early warning system for us.

39

Throw me a fricking de Bono

A sideways look at lateral thinking techniques.

Three switches outside a windowless room
are connected to three lightbulbs inside
the room. Can you determine which
switch is connected to which bulb if you are
only allowed to enter the room once?

The answer? I'll tell you in a minute. But first a story.

Two men were on a jungle safari in Africa. Suddenly, they came across a tiger that started roaring. Both men were frightened and one of them started putting on a pair of trainers. The other man said: 'How's that going to help? We can't outrun the tiger.'

The first man replied: 'I don't have to outrun the tiger, I only have to outrun you.'

OK, here's the answer to the light bulb puzzle: switch on the first switch and leave it on for a minute before switching it off again. Then switch on the second switch and enter the room. The second switch will be connected to the light that is on, the first switch will be connected to the light with the warm bulb, and the third switch will be connected to the light with the cold bulb.

Here's an idea for you... **Identify a challenge you face over the next few weeks – buying a birthday present, applying for a job, saving money for a holiday and so on. Ask yourself how most people might tackle that challenge and then commit yourself to coming up with a different approach.**

If these examples are new to you, perhaps your reaction to discovering the payoff was similar to mine when I first came across them – a Homer Simpsonesque 'doh' followed by a mildly grudging acknowledgement that it was a fair mental cop.

Both of these examples demonstrate the art of 'lateral thinking', a term coined by Edward de Bono, a leading authority in the field of creative and conceptual thinking back in 1967. On his website (www.edwdebono.com/), de Bono offers a number of ways of viewing lateral thinking. To take a couple of examples:

You cannot dig a hole in a different place by digging the same hole deeper: this means that trying harder in the same direction may not be as useful as changing direction. Effort in the same direction will not necessarily succeed.

Lateral thinking is for changing concepts and perceptions: with logic you start out with certain ingredients, just as in playing chess you start out with given pieces. But what are those pieces? In most real life situations the pieces are not given, we just assume they are there. We assume certain perceptions, certain concepts and certain boundaries. Lateral thinking is concerned not with playing with the existing pieces but with seeking to change those very pieces. It is concerned with the perception part of thinking. This is where we organise the external world into the pieces that we can then 'process'.

To be a successful lateral thinker, we need to become alert to the assumptions we make when we assess a situation. You may recall the old chestnut that trainers like to trot out from time to time – you know the one: Don't ASSUME because assuming makes an ASS out of U and ME. Laugh, I never did.

IDEA 5, *Buddy, can you spare a paradigm?*, goes into assumption testing in more detail.

Try another idea...

The difficulty with assumptions is that a lot of the time they serve a very useful purpose by providing us with a mental shorthand for dealing with the world. We assume, for example, that the world is round. We don't question the matter. OK, so the world *is* round, and so it's a reasonable basis on which to make decisions and choices. The point is, though, that, not so long ago, it was widely accepted that the world was flat and that it was literally possible to sail off the end of the world.

Before we chortle too heartily at the ignorance of our predecessors, here's a question: What are we assuming to be true today, that is or might

'Either he's dead or my watch has stopped.'
GROUCHO MARX

Defining idea...

turn out to be a wrong assumption? Peter Senge, populariser of the learning organisation concept, believes that we often limit our capacity to learn because we weave webs of assumptions within which we become our own victims. The box, outside of which we are often encouraged to think, is actually a box of assumptions.

'The play was a great success but the audience was a disaster.'
OSCAR WILDE

Defining idea...

When confronting a lateral thinking puzzle, we can safely assume that, to use the old cliché, there is more to it than meets the eye. If we start engaging all our other senses as well, then we'll have a much richer sensory base from which to investigate the world.

How did it go?

Q **I've had a go at a few lateral thinking puzzles but can't help thinking that they're no more than amusing diversions. Am I right, or is there more to them than that?**

A *Yes, there certainly is more to them than just a bit of idle brain stretching. Lateral thinking puzzles remind us that it is useful to test out assumptions from time to time to see if they still hold true. These puzzles also invite us to go beyond the explicit information we are given and to draw on our wider body of knowledge about the world: we know from watching countless wildlife programmes that tigers kill their prey one at a time; we also know that light bulbs get hot after they've been on for a few moments. When we are thinking laterally, we have to think more richly and with greater sensory perception than we normally do.*

Q **But do we really benefit from being able to think laterally?**

A *At one level we are just enjoying a mental teaser. But lateral thinking offers other benefits. It teaches us to constructively challenge, and it helps us to develop a mindset that looks to solve problems in ways that don't initially come to mind. Both of these benefits can serve us well in our personal and work lives.*

40

Bring your body up to scratch

Here's the low-down on the connection between physical and mental health and what you might need to do to give your brain the body it deserves.

Nobody in their right mind would put a Rolls Royce car engine under the bonnet of a clapped out Ford Cortina and expect top-class performance. The same principle applies to putting Einstein's brain in the body of, say, a late-period Elvis Presley.

Before the more pedantic of this book's readership put pen to paper to point out that nowadays Einstein's brain exists only in small pieces floating around pickling jars in all four corners of the planet, and would therefore be of little use inside the head of the fittest person that humanity could muster, let alone in Elvis's, know this: I'm not being literal, I'm making a point, namely that our physical state and our mental performance are linked.

That's not to say an overweight person cannot possess a searing intelligence, or that a physically perfect specimen will automatically be blessed with genius. But for the majority of us, the better our state of fitness, the more likely we are to think optimally.

Here's something to dispel the idea that we are masters of our own bodies. You can try this sitting at your desk. Lift your right foot off the floor and make clockwise circles. Now, while doing this, draw the number '6' in the air with your right hand. Your foot will change direction and there's nothing you can do about it.

And yet, despite the exhortations of the nation's doctors and other health professionals, it's estimated that around 75 per cent of the UK adult population do not exercise enough to show a health benefit. And this is before the full sedentary impact of the knowledge economy is felt.

We are in danger of becoming a nation of couch potatoes. Actually, it is a sign of the times that British potato farmers carried out protests recently in a bid to get the term 'couch potato' removed from the *Oxford English Dictionary* on the grounds that the phrase is derogatory and misrepresents potatoes.

Anyway, what has become increasingly clear is that we generally eat more than we need to and exercise less than we should. Part of the problem is that modern life can reduce the opportunities for us to build up a bit of a sweat in the normal course of a day. We drive rather than walk, we work in jobs that are more about mental exertion rather than physical, and we use labour-saving devices (and for labour-saving, read calorie-retaining) like the vacuum cleaner rather than clean the house with a spoon (OK, I'm getting silly now, but you get my drift).

However we choose to get fit, there are a number of benefits that result from taking regular exercise.

The health benefits of exercise include a decreased resting heart rate, reduced blood pressure and improved insulin sensitivity. Our increased blood flow and oxygenation can give our skin a healthy glow. The increased energy level combined with the increased glandular output results in increased sexuality.

The psychological benefits are that exercise:

- improves our sense of well-being and enhances our self-image, partly by enabling us to see positive physical change in ourselves ('Oh look, there are my feet. Haven't seen them in ages because they were hiding behind my beer gut.')

- stimulates the nervous system to make us feel more alert

- decreases anxiety and tension by creating an outlet from daily tension and anxiety

- reduces depression (exactly why, we're not sure, but scientists believe that enhancing body image, elevating moods and improving our general health and physical appearance can all help boost self-esteem and self-confidence)

You can find more on how healthy eating feeds into a wider maintenance regime in IDEA 26, *Feed your head.*

Try another idea...

'I may have the body of a weak and feeble woman, but I have the heart and stomach of a concrete elephant.'
QUEENIE, from the TV series *Blackadder II*

Defining idea...

■ enhances adherence to weight control behaviours, or to put it another way, the more we exercise and see positive results, the more we want to carry on exercising

Scientists tell us that when we are exercising, we generate chemicals called endorphins (actually, an abbreviation of the phrase endogenous morphine, in other words how morphine is produced naturally by the body and released into the system) body. Endorphins are thought to relieve stress and pain naturally, giving the person exercising that euphoric and invigorating feeling sometimes known as runner's high.

Defining idea...

'Fitness - If it came in a bottle, everybody would have a great body.'
CHER

However we choose to take our exercise, the important thing is that we fit it into our lives somehow. So if you're one of the millions who could usefully take more exercise, what are you going to do about it?

Q   I've been casting an eye over the lifestyle of my teenage children. It's sometimes said that people now in their teens and twenties belong to the first generation whose level of fitness compares badly with the previous generation. Is this true?

How did it go?

A   *Research does seem to support this view. Part of the problem seems to be that, unlike previous generations, for whom exercise was to a degree a natural by-product of everyday life, many people today need to consciously engineer exercise opportunities into their lives.*

Q   What can be done to tackle this state of affairs?

A   *As I say, we need to engineer exercise back into our lives, either by incorporating it into our normal routines (by walking or cycling to work, for example) or by setting aside time specifically for exercise (by joining a health club or going for a regular jog). As we move more and more into knowledge work and away from physical labour, the importance of taking exercise grows.*

179

41

Be a first-class conversationalist

Meeting and talking with others can be a brilliant way to hone your thinking as well as your ability to express yourself clearly. So it's time for some pointers on the art of conversation.

Sometimes we meet somebody for the first time and we just click with them. The conversational juices flow, nay gush.

When that happens, it's wonderful. Sometimes, though, we need to put a bit of effort into making the conversation work. It's worth doing, though, because every time we meet somebody, we have an opportunity to learn about them and their world-view, and to expand our own views, knowledge and perceptions.

So here are some pearls of wisdom that should help us improve our hit rate when it comes to conversing successfully. Funnily enough, the work starts well before we meet up with somebody:

Here's an idea for you... **If you want to show somebody that you *really* have been paying attention to them, a brilliant conversational gambit is to go beyond what they have just been talking about and to pick up something they mentioned earlier in the conversation. It's a strong signal to the other party that you've been paying attention and moves the conversation to a deeper, more engaged level.**

PREPARATION

Read widely: everything you read can be a source of conversation.

Immerse yourself in culture, both high and low – TV, music, sports, fashion, art, the theatre – all are great sources of chat. If you can't stand Shakespeare or rap music or football, that too can be a good topic for talk.

Keep a note of funny stories you hear, beautiful things you see, quotes, observations, shopping lists and calls you made.

Expand your horizons: go home a new way; try sushi; visit new places; learn a musical instrument; find a good website. Anything that you've just got into is grist to the conversational mill.

Practise. The more you converse, the more at ease you become. Get into the habit of conversing with people: cashiers, waiters, colleagues, neighbours, and so on.

THE CONVERSATION ITSELF

Look interested in the other person and what he or she has to say. Give off some minimal encouragers: these are those small signals that people put out to indicate that they're fully engaged in the conversation – nodding the head, smiling and other facial reactions, and brief verbal signals ('uh huh', 'yeah', 'really?'). These work best when they are natural, unforced responses. Used to excess, they become at best a distracting mannerism and at worst faintly sinister or an indication that you're taking the piss.

Respond to what he or she has just said ('Oh, really? Why do you say that?', 'Tell me more') or just repeat with a quizzical lilt the last part of the previous sentence – 'the last part of the previous sentence?' Yes, that's right, it shows that you're listening and so encourages the speaker to keep talking.

THINGS TO WATCH OUT FOR

Show a little sensitivity: when somebody has gone a little moist-eyed upon sharing the news of the demise of a beloved pet, the appropriate response is not 'So who's going to win Big Brother this year then?'

Try to be alert to your conversational mannerisms. Watch out for words or phrases you use time and time again – 'basically', 'at the end of the day', and so on.

There's nothing wrong with having a few polished anecdotes up your sleeve to rattle off if the moment is right. But keep yourself reined in a bit – a snappy, well told anecdote is one thing, launching into a twenty-minute recital of the Beowulf legend is something entirely different.

Want to spice up your conversations with a few witty remarks? Go to IDEA 23, *Take a walk on the Wilde side.*

Try another idea...

183

Defining idea...

'A single conversation across the table with a wise person is worth a month's study of book.'
Chinese proverb

Keep within boundaries – to begin with at least: unless you know the other person well already, don't go sharing details of your sex life within thirty seconds of meeting. Too much, too soon.

Pretentious, moi? Your quips in Latin and scientific discourses will be wasted on some.

Follow the conversation to a natural end-point and then disengage. Don't let your conversation degenerate until it reaches that tumbledown-blowing-by moment when you're both reduced to absolute silence.

To sum up, a good conversation is:

- a balance between talking and listening

- a genuine exchange of views and information, not a monologue

- a mix of the spontaneous and the semi-rehearsed

- an opportunity to learn (and remember that we learn more when we're listening than when we're talking)

So go on: hone those anecdotes and perfect that nod. Now go out and meet somebody new.

Q **I sometimes struggle to end a conversation with style – any tips on how to manage that sweet sorrow that is parting?**

How did it go?

A *Your heart's in the right place if your aim is to break off from conversation in a way that leaves both of you feeling OK. You might want to try a three-step exit: one, appreciate the conversation; two, give a rationale for ending the conversation; and three, anticipate another meeting in the future. Here's an example that follows the structure: 'It's been lovely to meet you. Thanks for the wonderful chat, but there's somebody I needed to catch and it looks like they're on the point of leaving. Catch you later.'*

Q **I always plan to have a good-quality conversation when I meet up with people but all too often things seem to descend into a gossip-fixated chinwag. Any advice on how I can raise the tone of my conversation?**

A *Somebody once said that conversation is an exercise of the mind and gossip is an exercise of the tongue. There's nothing wrong with a bit of a gossip from time to time, but it doesn't exactly improve the mind. To keep the quality of conversation up, be prepared to introduce topics as well as to respond to what the other person is saying. The more you can lead the conversation, the more you can steer things in the direction you choose.*

42

OK, repeat after me....

If you can't sum up what somebody has just said, you either weren't paying proper attention or you didn't understand their point. Time for a crash course in the neglected arts of listening and summarising.

We think we listen, but actually we don't most of the time. Instead, we finish the other person's sentences for them, interrupt, steal glances at our watches, and think about what to eat or who to ring that evening.

Good listening skills are the bedrock of good decision making, effective networking, seeing the big picture, managing information, etc. In fact, listening is essential for most life and business skills – yet the art of how to listen is barely given any time at all in our education system. Perhaps educators assume that it's on a par with breathing – just something we are automatically good at.

For whatever reason, there's a real scarcity of good listeners around, and, in the absence of good role models, bad listening habits perpetuate themselves in a free-for-all talk-fest.

Here's an idea for you... **Think about how you feel on the next few occasions when you are interrupted by somebody else. Are you pleased they interrupted? Do you feel miffed? Are you concerned that you must be boring them? Are they better at finishing your sentence than you are? Now try making a point of not interrupting people when they are speaking. How does that feel?**

If we are serious about wanting to upgrade our thinking skills, we have to ask ourselves a critical question: Am I more likely to learn by speaking or by listening? Both, of course, play their part, but as somebody – no idea who – once remarked, we have two ears and one mouth and so we should aim to listen and talk in similar proportions.

How do you become a good listener? Here are a few tips:

Maintain eye contact with the person you're listening to, and try to look interested in what is being said. Remember, you listen with your face and your body, not just with your ears. If you feel your mind wandering, change the position of your body and try to concentrate on what the speaker is saying.

Try to focus on the words, rather than any quirks in delivery, such as accent, or verbal or physical tics.

Don't let your mind become distracted by external occurrences – a noisy air-conditioning unit, an attractive person of the gender of your choice walking by, and so on.

Wait for the speaker to pause before asking clarifying questions. Try repeating in your own words what the speaker said so that you can check whether your understanding is correct.

Pay attention to what isn't said – to feelings, facial expressions and other nonverbal cues. Be particularly alert to apparent discrepancies between the words and the body language.

Listening is the natural bedfellow of talking, so to learn more about speaking your mind, have a look at IDEA 21, It's good to talk.

Try another idea...

Don't interrupt and don't jump in too soon – the speaker might be pausing to reflect, or even to breath.

On a related note, let yourself finish listening before you start speaking. If you respond too quickly, it suggests that you've been formulating what you want to say rather than taking in what has been said.

Listen out particularly for the main ideas or points that the speaker wants to get across. Phrases such as 'My point is...' or 'The thing to remember is...' are key moments when the speaker is distilling or reflecting on something that is clearly important in his view.

High-quality listening is an active process that has two key steps: hearing and understanding. Hearing means listening well enough to catch what the speaker is saying. Understanding is your ability to appreciate what the other person means. Can you, for instance, sum up the key points made in a few sentences?

Good-quality listening also requires both commitment and restraint: commitment to wanting to understand the other person's point of view; and restraint in terms of not be overly interventionist.

'*He knew the precise psychological moment when to say nothing.*'
OSCAR WILDE

Defining idea...

How did it go?

Q **I was talking with somebody the other day who suddenly accused me of not paying attention to what she was saying. Actually I was taking it in – I guess I was just not giving off the right signals. What can I do?**

A *You need to give the speaker visual and verbal feedback to show that you really are paying attention. Aim to keep good eye contact going, look interested, nod to indicate understanding, summarise, reflect feelings, and say 'mmm' or 'yeah' from time to time. Don't overdo it, though – the occasional lowish key 'yeah' is fine, a full-blooded Austin Powers-like 'yeah, baby!' after the other party completes each sentence will prove a tad off-putting.*

Q **To tell you the truth, sometimes I don't really pay attention. My mind just seems to drift off. What can I do?**

A *It's always possible that you are listening to a very dull person with nothing to say and so you might not be missing much anyway! On the other hand, it could be a problem with concentration. If you definitely want to pay attention, periodically ask yourself if you could summarise what the other person has just said. Then occasionally feed it back to the other person as a double-check. Another thing to try is to develop a saying or phrase that will help you snap to attention if you catch yourself wandering. You don't say this out loud by the way. I have a friend who uses the phrase 'Right here, right now' to bring himself right back into the moment.*

43

Cut the crap

If your brain has ever become befuddled by information overload, here are a few ideas for clearing excess data out of your life.

Remember Sisyphus, the king in Greek mythology who was condemned by the gods to forever roll a big rock to the top of a mountain, only to have it roll back down again? Lucky bastard.

Same rock, same mountain – I call that nice regular work. No, it's us I feel sorry for. Condemned to be forever shipping emails out of our inbox only for the box to fill again by the next morning. It's like giving the engine room crew on the Titanic a spoon to keep the ship afloat with.

Information overload is one of the less attractive by-products of the knowledge economy. Researchers from Berkeley have estimated that the amount of information stored globally has been growing at the rate of 30 per cent a year for the last 10 years. That statistic doesn't surprise me at all. When I last checked, there were over 20 million websites out there, and literally thousands of magazines and books published every week. Add to that the year-on-year growth in junk mail invading our homes, and it's small wonder that we struggle to deal with it all without succumbing to a dose of the screaming abdabs.

Here's an idea for you...

When you are in email correspondence with someone, consider changing the words in the subject field rather than just let it become a series of 'Re:'s. Making a change can reflect how the conversation has moved on, so the recipient can decide whether to read the message now, later or not at all.

It's a real problem, and one that is not likely to go away. Overload can cause stress, which leads to a feeling of strain, and increases the likelihood of our mistakes. And a reputation for making mistakes is definitely not what we want in either our professional or our personal life – which adds to the stress...

What's clear is that we need to be smart about how we handle information. Here then are just a few ideas for clearing excess data out of your life:

- Review whether you actually read the newspapers and magazines you buy. See if you can reduce your intake.

- Tear out the magazine articles and news items that you really want to read and throw away the rest of the publication. That way, you don't risk unintentionally reading the same useless stuff again.

- Learn how to use search engines efficiently. Most have help sections that will teach you how to search to best effect. Check out some of the advanced features – they definitely can reduce the number of hits you get and thus give you a more focused set of results.

- Rather than continually visiting your favourite websites, see if they offer an RSS (Really Simple Syndication) service. This will notify you whenever the web pages that you specify are updated. Or why not go the whole hog and set up a personalised news reader?

- Seek out 'trusted filters', i.e. high-quality people, journals or websites that you can rely on to give you the distilled essence on subjects that you have an interest in.

To help stop you from adding to other people's overload, have a look at IDEA 4, *Get to the point*. 'Nuff said?

Try another idea...

- Where possible, go for the 'edited highlights' rather than the 'live transmission'. Watching a breaking news story on a 24-hour news channel can be highly amusing as we watch increasingly desperate news anchors and on-the-spot reporters stretch about 30 seconds of hard content over 15 minutes of broadcasting, but it's not the best use of our time. Far better to seek out a more considered newspiece once the story has played out.

- Consider getting hold of some time-shifting technology so that you can watch TV programmes at a time to suit you. This also gives you the opportunity to fast forward through the adverts and the boring bits.

- Avoid attending meetings where possible – make do with reading the minutes.

- Every six months or so, make a point of reviewing the amount of information you are handling and ask yourself whether there is scope to reduce your intake.

There is one critical point to remember. The purpose of reducing your information overload is not necessarily so that you can replace one set of information with a different set. Genuinely aim to reduce the amount of time dealing with this aspect of your life. After all, there must be something else you would rather be spending your time on.

'There is a real temptation that the thing that comes in the latest is the one you shift your attention to, even though that may be the least important.'
BILL GATES

Defining idea...

193

How did it go?

Q **I can manage the clutter in most parts of my life, but I do have a problem keeping on top of my emails. What can I do?**

A *Here are a few things you might try. (1) Set your email program to filter your emails. (2) Train yourself to ignore junk emails and unsolicited messages. You might miss the odd useful thing, but in the long run you'll be more focused and effective. (3) Don't leave any messages just sitting in your inbox – taking immediate action will prevent you from opening the same messages more than once.*

Q **Now I'm on top of my emails – it's just my work area that's a mess. Can't I leave it for another day?**

A *It really should be a priority to sort this out. Physical clutter is a constant distraction. Keep your work area clear of jumbled up piles. Don't simply file stuff away or put it in a drawer – the goal is to have less around altogether.*

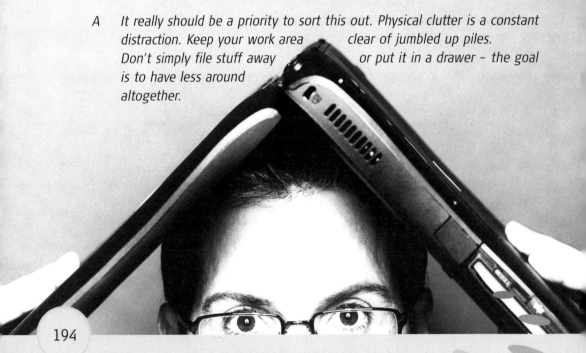

44

Pick a card, but not any card

You make your best decisions when you have choice, but not too much choice. So what can you do to effectively manage life's choice-points?

If you have ever considered a Chinese takeaway, did your heart leap joyously at the heady abundance of options set out in the menu? Or did having that many choices cause you a wave of unease possibly bordering on mild hysteria?

Whatever your reaction, the array of options in a takeaway menu can seem positively spartan compared with what confronts us in other parts of our lives.

For example, when I put the phrase 'things to do this weekend' into Google earlier today, I came up over 16 million hits. Even refining the search to 'things to do this weekend in the UK' still got well over three million results.

Here's another example: there are around 100,000 new books published each year in the UK. Even the most avid reader would struggle to get anywhere near reading 1 per cent of the choices on offer (that's three a day).

Here's an idea for you...

Learn to switch between satisficing and maximising. Both have their time and place. It's more important to select the right life partner than the best choice on a restaurant menu. So don't sweat over the small stuff.

Here's an idea for you...

'[The] fact that some choice is good doesn't necessarily mean that more choice is better...There is a cost to having an overload of choice. As a culture, we are enamoured of freedom, self-determination, and variety, and we are reluctant to give up any of our options. But clinging tenaciously to all the choices available to us contributes to bad decisions, to anxiety, stress, and dissatisfaction – even to clinical depression.'
BARRY SCHWARTZ, academic and author

Psychologist Barry Schwartz, author of *The Paradox of Choice*, believes that having so much choice isn't necessarily good for us. Because of the growing number of options we are presented with in so many facets of our lives, we don't always have the time to look at all the information out there to make the best choice.

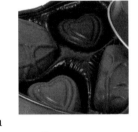

Dr Schwartz asks us to think about the difference between the best and good enough. He suggests that there are two types of decision makers: one group, which he calls *maximisers*, are people who want the absolute best. They have to examine every choice or they fear that they are not making the most of their opportunities. However, some people take the view that life's too short, so we shouldn't obsess over making choices. It's too frustrating and time-consuming to look at all the choices on offer. He calls people in this second category *satisficers*: these are people who look at some of the options and choose one that might not be the best but is good enough.

Generally speaking, says Schwartz, we should strive to be satisficers rather than maximisers, because satisficers are usually happy with the choice they have made. In contrast, maximisers often come to regret their decision.

For more on whittling down a lot of choices to a more manageable number, investigate IDEA 2, *Solve it like Sherlock.*

Try another idea...

Of course, some decisions are more significant than others. A typical supermarket carries more than 30,000 different items. When we go to do the weekly food shop, we are typically buying goods that don't cost very much and which will be consumed within a few days. So buying, for example, the wrong brand of cookies doesn't have huge emotional or financial consequences for us, because we can buy the different brand next time. However, in many other settings, we are out to buy things that cost more money, and that are meant to last. And here, as the number of options increases, the psychological stakes rise accordingly.

So how can we make the best possible decision about something important?

Well, we can sift through as many options as we are able to, and then in our own time make the best decision we can, considering all the available options we are aware of at the time. Having decided, we act.

At this point, for the sake of our mental well-being as much as anything, we need to live with our choice – for the time being anyway. We might consciously decide to review the decision at some point in the future, but we won't beat ourselves up in the meantime if it looks like better options may have become available.

'Less is more.'
ROBERT BROWNING, as built upon by Ludwig Mies van der Rohe, architect

Defining idea...

The important thing is to recognise that, most of the time, we won't find a solution that is best in class both now and for any length of time into the future. So let's get used to the idea. As Clint Eastwood famously said in one of his Dirty Harry movies, 'A man's got to know his limitations.'

How did it go?

Q   **I'm quite happy to make my own mind up where I can, but sometimes there aren't enough hours in the day to do that. Is there an alternative?**

A   *You might want to consider adopting the 'Trusted Friend' strategy. This involves ceding all or part of a decision to somebody else to make for us. In the health care field, for example, we expect the doctor to tell us what kind of treatment we need. When it comes to making big financial decisions, perhaps we should leave it to experts who can filter the available choices and recommend either one specific option to us or possibly a shortlist of choices if there is no clear-cut best buy.*

Q   **I can see how that could work. But what about if I want to make the decisions off my own bat?**

A   *With the 'Trusted Friend' strategy, you do retain the right to accept or refuse the recommendation. The main benefit is that you are getting other people to draw up the shortlist for you.*

45

Ain't nothing like the real thing

Time for a look at the different levels at which reality can be defined, and why this is a matter of practical concern.

A little while back, I came across a fascinating, if baffling, theory that a multitude of not-quite-identical copies of our universe exist, all of which are as real as our own. Relax — that's not what this Idea is about.

Nor is this a philosophical treatise concerning the nature of reality and truth. For now, let's assume that I exist (probably) and, of course, you do too.

My intentions here are rather more pragmatic. You remember that old conundrum about whether the glass is half-full or half-empty? One answer, I seem to recall from my student days, is that it depends on who is buying the next round.

The point is that we humans see the same things but draw different conclusions about their meaning. You go to a movie with a friend – you love it, they hate it. It's not that either of you is right or wrong (although I maintain to this day that

Here's an idea for you...

Over the next week, try to notice how people seamlessly switch between external reality, social reality and individual reality when they speak. You'll see how fact and perception are intertwined. Then, before you start feeling at all smug, start noticing how much you do it too.

Footloose is a great film). My view of the world makes sense to me – your view, I daresay, makes absolute sense to you.

The same goes for our behaviour. Everything I do is entirely logical and reasonable in my eyes. Ditto for you with your behaviour. If I don't understand why you do or don't do a particular thing – change jobs, dump your partner, go to the gym, or whatever – it's not that your behaviour is objectively illogical, it's just that I don't understand your internal universe.

To help us understand how each of us sees the world in different ways and then attaches different meanings to our experiences, let's have a go at grasping the nettle and tackle the big question: what is reality?

I know at this point we risk entering a philosophical and conceptual quagmire, but please accept for now that there are three different types of reality, namely:

Defining idea...

'Perception is real – even when it is not reality.'
EDWARD DE BONO

- external reality
- social reality
- individual reality

External reality refers to that which is determined empirically by objective tests. So, for example, mountains are real, the Sydney Harbour Bridge is real, elephants and bananas are real. They all have a physical reality such that nobody could reasonably dispute their existence. Try ignoring an elephant that's just trod on your foot if you don't believe me.

Social reality refers to those things that groups agree are matters of consensus, rather than things that are empirically testable. Collectively held assumptions about the meaning of life, religion and culture are

> For a few pointers on revealing what's really not real, pop along to IDEA 5, *Buddy, can you spare a paradigm?*

Try another idea...

examples of social reality. If a group of people agree to define something as real, it effectively becomes real for that group. Chelsea's football supporters doubtless think their team is the bee's knees; ask a group of Manchester United supporters for their view of Chelsea and you'll get a different story.

When companies describe their corporate culture as 'the way we do things around here', they are describing a social reality, not an external reality. That said, anybody who has

> *'One man's ceiling is another man's floor.'*
> PAUL SIMON

Defining idea...

ever joined a company only to find that they don't really gel with the prevailing culture may well have found that, while the social reality isn't really real, some of the penalties for non-conformance – demotion, job loss, exclusion – are very tangible and have a significant practical impact.

Individual reality is about what one person takes to be true based on their experience and knowledge of the world. Critically, this truth may not be shared by others. Edgar Schein, a professor at MIT, believes that individual reality is the least negotiable, or hardest to change, of the three types of reality. Once we as individuals get an idea or a viewpoint fixed in our head as true, it's very difficult for us to let it go.

> *'For there is nothing either good or bad, thinking makes it so.'*
> WILLIAM SHAKESPEARE

Defining idea...

201

This is particularly true in today's society, where respect for authority is not what it was. We are no longer inclined to believe something simply because our monarch/head of state/headteacher tells us it is so. As society becomes increasingly pragmatic and individualistic in outlook, we have replaced deference to authority figures with an outlook that says, in effect, 'prove it to me'.

All of which brings me to sharing with you the question that will give you and others the best possible grip on reality. When you hear somebody stating an opinion as though it were fact, simply ask them: how do you know this to be true?

How did it go?

Q   Levels of reality? I haven't inadvertently wandered onto the film set of *The Matrix*, have I? Does this stuff have any practical application?

A   *Yes, it does. We need to recognise the three different levels of reality and how they play out in our daily lives. These levels help to explain why, for example, we feel or think differently from our parents. They also highlight why the people who work for us, not to mention our children, don't accept our authority automatically. They have their own perceptions of what is and isn't real for them.*

Q   So if we are dealing with people who are working with different realities to our own, what can we do to bridge the gap?

A   *These days, logic and reason, not power and authority, are the tools by which we achieve our ends – managerial, parental or whatever. But even logic and reason will only work if we understand and work with other people's experience bases, and stop assuming that they are carbon copies of us.*

46

Become a core competent

If you want to be smart, build up your knowledge base. Tomorrow's world belongs to the 'core competents'.

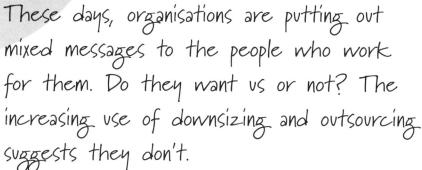

These days, organisations are putting out mixed messages to the people who work for them. Do they want us or not? The increasing use of downsizing and outsourcing suggests they don't.

A survey in 1999 from the Institute of Directors and Development Dimensions International asked HR directors what percentage of their employees they would rehire if they could change all their employees overnight. Half said they would rehire between 0 and 40 per cent.

On the other hand, as the late management guru Peter Drucker put it: 'In the knowledge society the most probable assumption for organizations – and certainly the assumption on which they have to conduct their affairs – is that they need knowledge workers far more than knowledge workers need them.'

Of course, these mixed messages are reconcilable. Organisations want some, but not all, of us, and organisations only want us badly if they perceive us to be a source of added value. In short, we are in an era of conditional corporate love.

Here's an idea for you...

Spend some time identifying an opportunity that you think will add value to your personal 'brand' in the career marketplace. For example, it might be a job move, getting on board with a high-profile organisational project, joining an organising committee, giving a conference speech, or writing an article for your professional journal – anything that gets your card marked as somebody to watch. Now go and do your level best to make it happen!

Against this backdrop, those of us who want to build a substantial career within organisations need to develop for ourselves (and regularly reinvent) a pool of skills and knowledge that will justify our place in a company's shrinking set of vital functions. To put it another way, we need to become one of what writer Stuart Crainer calls one of an organisation's 'Core Competents'.

Core competents are the small number of people in an organisation who are absolutely vital to that organisation's success. Bill Gates has said that there are 20 people who are absolutely pivotal to Microsoft, and that the company would risk bankruptcy or a severe dip in the share price at the very least if they were to leave. In a study by the Corporate Leadership Council, a computer firm identified 100 core competents out of 16,000 employees; a software company had 10 out of 11,000; and a transportation group reckoned that 20 of its 33,000 staff were absolutely critical to the company.

So what sort of steps can we take to build our personal knowledge base and hence increase our value in the marketplace? Here are a few tips:

- Develop career purpose – people with a vision of the future and goals linked to that vision are far more likely to succeed than those who don't.

- Be visible – find ways to raise your profile.

- Network like crazy.

- Think ahead: taking care of your job is not the same as taking care of your career. To avoid career inertia, schedule in regular reviews of where you and your career are heading.

For more on excelling at what you do, see IDEA 31, *Excel is not just a spreadsheet.*

Try another idea...

The crucial thing is that we should never become complacent about our knowledge levels. The skills, knowledge and experience that got us where we are today will not

be enough to get us where we might want to be tomorrow. So we need to consciously set out to maintain and build on our current knowledge base, as well as to acquire new skills and knowledge. Then, as the icing on the knowledge cake, we need to start thinking about what to do when those new skills and knowledge themselves become obsolete.

So spend some time thinking about how you can build your personal intellectual capital. Assuming you will need to earn money for a few years yet, what is your game plan for being valued highly in your chosen marketplace in one year's time? How about three years? And five? Bearing in mind that some knowledge-building activities take time to achieve – pursuing formal qualifications, for example – what do you need to start focusing on now to be where you want to be in the future?

'We are moving into an economy where the greatest value is in the recipes rather than the cakes.'
CHARLES LEADBEATER

Defining idea...

205

Above all, trust your own judgement: by all means, take regular soundings of other people's views about where the world of work is heading, but be sure to make up your own mind. In these volatile times, don't rely on anybody else's view of the future.

How did it go?

Q   I'm struggling with the terminology a bit here. Is a knowledge worker the same as a core competent?

A   *You've got the gist of it. Think of a core competent as an elite knowledge worker if you will.*

Q   That's helpful but I do find this all a bit conceptual. What can I do in practical terms to build up my knowledge base?

A   *How specifically any of us chooses to build up our knowledge base is largely down to our preferred ways of learning. For some, it could mean pursuing a qualification; others might opt for a more practical approach – like seeking out a secondment. But the important thing is that we do what we have to to continue to be relevant to whichever market we choose to be in. Peter Drucker rightly identified that knowledge confers tremendous power on those who possess it; the downside is that if our skills and knowledge fall out of date, then the market will ruthlessly abandon us.*

Develop a Plan B

Nineteenth-century scientist Louis Pasteur once said chance favours the prepared mind, so what would you do if disaster struck tomorrow – at home, at work, or anywhere come to that?

There's no real knowing what tomorrow holds for us. As movie mogul Sam Goldwyn once famously said: 'It's difficult to make predictions, especially about the future.'

At a time when we are facing unprecedented levels of change in just about every aspect of our lives, what can we do as individuals to increase our chances of coping effectively with whatever the future might throw at us?

We might learn something from the approach that companies take. Most medium-to-large organisations deal with managing the future in two distinct ways. First, they develop a strategic plan which sets out goals for the company and how those goals might be achieved. Underpinning this process is the need for real clarity about why the company exists in the first place and what its vision is for the future.

Secondly, companies increase their preparedness for dealing with unpredictable future events by developing a business recovery plan. This enables them to think through how they could resume normal service as quickly as possible after some level of disaster strikes.

Perhaps the challenge for us as individuals is to go through a similar process. First, we need a personal life strategy. This addresses questions like:

- Why are we here?

- What is our life's purpose?

- What are our overriding goals and dreams for the future?

- What targets should we be setting ourselves over the coming months and years?

- What do we need to be doing differently?

Here's an idea for you... **Imagine this: you lose your job tomorrow. Most jobs are filled through personal contacts, rather than through adverts in the papers and journals. So how good is your network? If it's poor, start building it up now rather than later. It takes time and effort to nurture and develop a network.**

Answering these questions can give our lives an overall sense of direction.

However, this in itself is not enough. Perhaps we should also give some thought to having our personal equivalent of a business recovery plan – a personal recovery plan if you will.

A personal recovery plan enables us to think through specifically how to deal with a number of potentially traumatic events – the loss of a job, loss of income, death of a parent or a dependant, or, come to that, our own death. Take a look at whatever circumstances you feel appropriate. And aim to be as detailed in your thinking as possible. It's not really adequate to plan for the potential loss of your job by just acknowledging that you would need to put together a new CV pronto and start trudging around the employment agencies. You need to be addressing issues like how marketable your skills are right now, whether the market is buoyant or flat, how the loss of your job would affect you financially. Once you've considered these issues, the pressing question becomes this: What should you be doing today and over the coming months to improve your ability to deal with that kind of eventuality?

For a few tips on how to prepare for the future, see IDEA 49, *Create multiple futures*.

Try another idea…

This, by the way, is a different process to scenario planning, where the focus tends to be on planning to deal with a range of alternative futures, any of which might come to pass.

'I never make predictions about the future. I never have and I never will.'
TONY BLAIR, possibly after spending too much time in the company of George Bush

Defining idea…

In truth, of course, nobody can be absolutely sure what the future holds. This is after all what social philosopher Charles Handy has call the age of unreason, a time 'when the future, in so many areas, is to be shaped by us and for us; a time when the only prediction that will hold true is that no predictions will hold true; a time therefore for bold imaginings…for thinking the unlikely and doing the unreasonable'.

In such times, it pays dividends to be infinitely resilient and infinitely adaptable. The challenge for each of us to is determine what that means in practice and what we need to do to achieve that state.

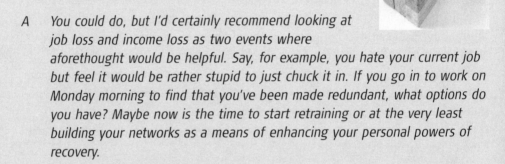

How did it go?

Q **I'm a busy person. Why do I need to develop a personal recovery plan? Can't I just deal with things on the day if the worst comes to the worst?**

A *You could do, but I'd certainly recommend looking at job loss and income loss as two events where aforethought would be helpful. Say, for example, you hate your current job but feel it would be rather stupid to just chuck it in. If you go in to work on Monday morning to find that you've been made redundant, what options do you have? Maybe now is the time to start retraining or at the very least building your networks as a means of enhancing your personal powers of recovery.*

Q **OK, so I've put together my personal recovery plan. Now what do I do with it?**

A *It should be a dynamic, changing document, so, for a start, you should pencil a date in your diary maybe six months or so down the line when you will review and update the contents. A good-quality personal recovery plan might also entail you taking some specific actions during the intervening months – perhaps you decide to start going along to meetings of your professional association, or possibly you might work on trying to arrange a secondment to a different part of the business for developmental reasons. The whole purpose of the document is to help you anticipate the future and to take steps now to be in the best possible position to face whatever comes your way.*

48

Nothing fails like success

Just because something works today doesn't mean it will work tomorrow. Every great idea contains the seeds of its own failure. Step one: recognise that. Step two: do something about it.

In the sporting games of ancient Greece — we're talking pre-Demis Roussos and even Nana Mouskouri here — the eventual victor in the competition was crowned with a laurel wreath.

But if the winner wanted to remain a champion, he could not afford to 'rest on his laurels'. Every athlete learns that a sure-fire way to go downhill from your peak is to stop training and just trade on past accomplishments. And even maintaining the same standard won't be enough to guarantee victory at the next games. The world moves on, standards improve and your competition overhauls you.

Nineteenth-century evolutionist Charles Darwin expressed this principle starkly; in effect, he said that if you can't evolve more quickly than your environment, then you're doomed.

Here's an idea for you... **Sit down and list your winning life strategies. Think about things like how you gain new friends, how you tackle exams, how you have succeeded in your career and so on – you may well find that you have recurring patterns that you deploy. Then consider how 'future-proof' these strategies are.**

Much more recently, musician, artist, producer and cultural theorist Brian Eno spoke of the temptation – one that he determinedly resists – to carry on replicating old familiar formulas rather than to innovate:

'There's a tremendously strong pressure to repeat yourself, to do more of that thing we all liked so much. I can't do that – I don't have the enthusiasm to push through projects that seem familiar to me (this isn't so much a question of artistic nobility or high ideals: I just get too bloody bored), but at the same time I do feel guilt for "deserting my audience" by not doing the things they apparently wanted.'

In the business world, writer and consultant Richard Pascale has described the ephemeral nature of success. According to Pascale, even if we manage to locate the formula for company success, it will be a formula with a sell-by date. He summed this phenomenon up with a memorable phrase: nothing fails like success.

Defining idea... **'Imitation is suicide.'**
RALPH WALDO EMERSON

Whether we choose to draw the lesson from the athletes of ancient Greece, from evolutionary theory, from the contemporary music scene or from the world of business, the message is startlingly similar: success is not self-maintaining. On the contrary, success has such a short shelf life these days that the very factors that bring us success today contain the seeds of our destruction tomorrow.

So the challenge for each of us is not to lapse into complacency when we achieve a level of success. Rather we need to develop a sense of 'divine discontent' – by all means recognising and revelling in our achievements, but also constantly striving to make the next leap forward.

Constantly testing your assumptions is a good way to ward off complacency. For more on this, have a look at IDEA 5, Buddy, can you spare a paradigm?

Try another idea...

So here are two key questions to think about:

Taking in all aspects of your life, what is working for you now perfectly well that you know in your heart of hearts won't work anything like as well in one year's time? This could be about your job, your relationships, your financial situation, the qualifications you currently hold, the level of knowledge you have about a particular subject, your current level of fitness and so on. It could even be about something as down to earth as the state of your car, your sash windows or your computer. The point is to be as thorough and as comprehensive as you can.

What do you need to do about the areas you've identified and when do you need to act? Having determined those areas of your life where a 'more of the same' strategy just won't deliver the goods, put together some form of action plan setting out when and how you plan to deal with the problem. A word of advice though – be careful who you let see your plans (it's not good if your partner gets to find out that you plan to dump him next May!)

'The significant problems that we face cannot be solved by the same level of thinking that created them.'
ALBERT EINSTEIN

Defining idea...

213

How did
it go?

Q **I've had a go at this but it does seem to be over-egging the pudding somewhat. Don't we have enough to worry about already without looking for problems?**

A *Admittedly, there is a very human temptation not to fix that which isn't broken. But that's to ignore a key truth that, whether in our work lives or our personal lives, conservatism kills. We need to be prepared to junk our current success formula if there are signs that it is beginning to fail us. Clinging to a formula simply because it has worked in the past is a recipe for the scrapheap. After all, you don't have to be ill to get better.*

Q **It seems a real shame, almost fickle in fact, to abandon a successful formula just because it has lost a little of its lustre. Is there no hope for it?**

A *Very occasionally the problem is not the formula, but rather the way the formula is being deployed. However, there are big dangers in trying to prop up the current approach, the main one being that familiarity and comfort with the current status quo blinds us to what might really be happening, which could be that the way we do things currently has had its day in the sun.*

49

Create multiple futures

When you don't know what the future holds, it makes sense to have a few options up your sleeve. 'Scenario planning' is a useful tool for improving our preparedness for the future.

Back in 1893, a number of prominent Americans were asked to predict what life would be like in 1993. The consensus view was that we would travel around in fast trains and air balloons, work only 3 hours a day, and live in houses made of aluminium.

This just goes to show that things rarely turn out as expected.

These days, trying to look 100 years ahead seems like a doomed pastime. In truth, who of us can predict with any confidence what's in store for us even 10 years down the line, when you consider the possible impact of biotechnology, nano-technology, globalisation, climate change and the like? The fact is that there's no absolute knowing where we might be heading over the next few years. The future has never been less predictable, be it at a global, national, organisational or personal level.

*Here's an
idea for
you...* **Make a list of the five worst
things that could happen to you
and then start developing a
reasonably detailed plan of
action for each one.**

Against that backdrop, we can take one of two
stances. There's the Doris Day school of
thought – 'que sera sera, whatever will be, will
be' – in other words, a vaguely fatalistic view of
the future where the strategy, if there is one, is
to deal with things as they happen. Then
there's the alternative approach: we don't know absolutely what's in store, but
those who know that something is coming are better prepared to face it than those
who don't. This is the basis for a technique called scenario planning, which involves
constructing a series of possible future realities and then examining the
ramifications of each scenario. The tool was developed for organisations to use, but
the principles work just as well for individuals.

In his book *The Art of the Long View*, Peter Schwartz, who led the scenario planning
unit at Royal/Dutch Shell for four years back in the early 1980s, describes how, in
practice, scenarios resemble a set of stories, written or spoken, built around carefully
constructed plots. 'Scenarios are stories that give meaning to events,' says Schwartz.
They are an old way of organising knowledge; when used as strategic tools, they
confront denial by encouraging – indeed, requiring – the willing suspension of
disbelief. Stories can express multiple perspectives on complex events.

Creating scenarios requires us to question our broadest assumptions about the way the world works. Good scenarios are plausible, surprising, and have the power to break old stereotypes. Using scenarios is 'rehearsing the future' such that, by recognising the warning signs, an organisation can adapt, and act effectively. As

If you really want to stretch your scenario-planning skills, have a look at IDEA 50, *Take the long view*, for a journey into the future that Doctor Who would be proud of.

Try another idea...

Schwartz puts it, 'Decisions which have been pre-tested against a range of what fate may offer are more likely to stand the test of time, produce robust and resilient strategies, and create distinct competitive advantage. Ultimately, the result of scenario planning is not a more accurate picture of tomorrow but better thinking…about the future.'

It's not always easy to get it right. Back in 2002, a friend of a friend who was going abroad for a couple of years decided to sell his house. He had seen a growing number of reports predicting an impending implosion of the property market causing steep drops in house prices, and he decided the canny thing to do would be to sell up and pocket the cash before the crash.

He was wrong. House prices continued to surge and he found on his return that his old house had risen in value by another 50 per cent while he had been away. Although his cash had gained a reasonable amount in interest, the upshot was that he couldn't afford to buy the house he had owned two years before.

'More than any other time in history, mankind faces a crossroad: one path leads to despair and hopelessness, and the other to total extinction. Let us pray we have the wisdom to choose correctly.' WOODY ALLEN

Defining idea...

The moral of this story is not that inaction is the best strategy; we shouldn't throw the decision-making baby out with the bad outcome bathwater. The moral is that managing our lives requires us to make choices and decisions about what might happen in the future.

The future may be unknowable, but it's not unmanageable. The more options and choices you have available, the better equipped you are to handle whatever the future throws at you. If you only have Plan A and maybe Plan B at a push, your options are very limited.

How did it go?

Q   I still don't get it. What's the point of scenario planning?

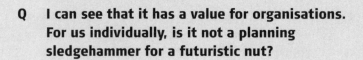

A   *Individuals and organisations use scenario planning in order to be prepared for all imaginable events. The main purpose of this process is to probe and challenge assumptions, and to ask some 'what if' questions. The outcome is better awareness and better preparedness.*

Q   I can see that it has a value for organisations. For us individually, is it not a planning sledgehammer for a futuristic nut?

A   *Not entirely. If we take the view that the future is unpredictable and essentially unknowable, then there is a value in creating a few contingency plans. For example, what if you are made redundant when you are 40? Or 50? Or 60? If, in that eventuality, you want to go for a complete change of career, are there steps you should be taking now to facilitate the transition? You could just wait and see and then muddle along the best you can through whatever life throws at you, but scenario planning offers a more proactive means of managing your future.*

50

Take the long view

In which yours truly has a bit of a rant about the shortcomings of short-termism and discusses the merits of having a weather eye on the temporal middle distance and beyond.

The law of cause and effect. I walk into a wall and bang my nose, next thing you know I'm sobbing and howling.

If I don't go to the shops in the next fifteen minutes, there will be nothing to eat tonight. If I don't book a table today, we won't be able to go to our favourite restaurant on Saturday evening. If I don't start writing my new book next month, it won't be finished in six months' time. If I don't sort out my pension situation this year, I'll have to go on working until I drop.

There is a reason why I'm sharing a chunk of my current to-do list with you, and that is to make the point that although we can only live and act in the here and now, a proportion of our thinking time every day has to be devoted to anticipating future events.

Most of the time, we are thinking just a few hours or a few days ahead, with only occasional effort expended on more medium- to long-term plans. Even then, we are much more likely to be thinking a few months ahead about a forthcoming holiday,

Here's an idea for you... **Build reflection time about the future into your monthly diary. Some plans take months, years, even decades to come to fruition. What do you need to start now to influence the long-term future?**

or an impending big birthday or anniversary rather than a few years ahead.

With that in mind, let me share with you a story:

The emperor had just moved into a new palace. He liked the palace and surrounding grounds but felt that something was missing. He summoned his head gardener.

The Emperor said to his gardener, 'We have some beautiful gardens here, but I think their appearance would be improved if we were to plant a double row of cedar trees running from the Summer House down to the lake.'

'Heavens above, your majesty,' the gardener replied. 'A double row of cedar trees will take a thousand years to grow.'

'In that case,' said the Emperor, 'we'd better make a start this afternoon. We haven't a moment to lose.'

Defining idea... **'Infinite gratitude for the past. Infinite service to the present. Infinite responsibility for the future.'**
Zen proverb

What an extraordinary thing – planning one thousand years ahead. But, as Bachman Turner Overdrive famously sang in their 1974 rock-tastic classic, 'You ain't seen nothing yet.'

Check out this mind-blowing view of the temporal scheme of things from physicist, mathematician and future-gazer Freeman Dyson:

'The destiny of our species is shaped by the imperatives of survival on six different time scales. To survive means to compete successfully on all six time scales. But the unit of survival is different on all six time scales.

- On a time scale of years, the unit is the individual.

- On a time scale of decades, the unit is the family.

- On a time scale of centuries, the unit is the tribe or the nation.

- On a time scale of millennia, the unit is the culture.

- On a time scale of tens of millennia, the unit is the species.

- On a time scale of eons, the unit is the whole web of life on our planet.'

To put it in a nutshell, we need to understand the long-term nature of some of the problems we face today. We must resist the urge to develop solutions that may only have a short-term effect.

Some people reading this are possibly thinking: But what can I do, there's only little old me? It's all too big. I can't think about it today, I'll think about it tomorrow. Fiddly dee.

While you are in the mood for looking into the future, check out IDEA 6, *Watch out for discontinuities*, which will help you develop an early warning system for what's around the corner.

Try another idea...

'We are the first generation that influences global climate, and the last generation to escape the consequences.'
Unnamed climatologist, quoted in *The Clock of the Long Now* by Stewart Brand

Defining idea...

Of course, if a then thirty-something Bob Geldof had succumbed to that kind of thinking in 1984, the world would never have witnessed Live Aid in 1985 and Live8 in 2005. Besides, if we collectively aren't responsible for the future of the planet, then who is?

How did it go?

Q   Is it remotely sensible to try to project our thinking so far into the future?

A   *It is challenging to do this, without a doubt, particularly when most of our attention is devoted to today, perhaps this week, with maybe just a lingering recall of last week. Think of taking the long view as some kind of temporal stretch target. We don't necessarily achieve a meaningful sense of one thousand years hence, but the process of thinking about it propels us into a whole new set of insights.*

Q   But how does all of this help us in a practical sense?

A   *Richard Pascale, academic and writer, came up with an interesting concept once. He called it 'managing the present from the future'. The idea is that once we have a vision of something we want to move to in the future, that vision impacts on our behaviour in the here and now. Remember the Emperor in the story, who needs action today in order to pursue his dream of having fully grown cedar trees in a thousand years' time. If we have a compelling sense of a future worth pursuing, it impacts very practically on our behaviour.*

Make it happen

Making it happen is about the desire to get on and take action, and to do so to a high standard. There's much more to life than giving yourself a gentle cerebral massage.

Let's confront a necessary if uncomfortable truth: knowledge without action is sterile; action without knowledge is blind. If the old enemy was mindset, the new enemy is inertia.

A friend of mine has a favourite four-letter acronym – JFDI – which, in the Parental Guidance version, stands for Just Flipping-well Do It. It's a call to arms of sorts, a recognition that there comes a point when the thinking and talking need to stop, and when ideas either turn into actions or regress back into mental mush.

So what's your track record like when it comes to making things happen? Are you an ace implementer who always follows plans through? Or are you somebody who's infinitely better at the talk than the walk – to use a phrase much loved by a colleague of mine, are you 'all mouth and no trousers'?

Most probably, you're selectively dynamic, i.e. sometimes you take effective action, sometimes you don't. If that's the case, you're welcome to join a not particularly select club sometimes better known as 'the vast majority of us'.

Here's an idea for you...

Once you have decided on a particular course of action, share your plans with somebody else. Declaring our intentions to others can lend real impetus to the process of making them happen. This probably works best when you're sharing plans face-to-face (it's pretty squirm-inducing having to tell your friends and colleagues you haven't done something you said you would). Increasingly, though, people use the internet as a means of sharing plans and supporting each other (I know of a group of people who operate a very successful weight loss club via phone and email).

Let's look at what's probably a familiar example. Think back to an occasion when you bumped into an old friend or acquaintance in the street that you hadn't seen in a while. Chances are that you had a perfectly pleasant, if brief, chat and then parted with both of you saying that it would be great to meet up for a coffee or a beer sometime soon. Assuming you weren't lying through your molars about wanting to see them again, did you take any kind of responsibility for ensuring that the follow-up latte took place?

If you're the sort of person who does habitually make sure that the next get-together happens, then you probably have the willpower, the energy and the organising skills to pick up a good idea

and run with it. If, on the other hand, you find that those get-togethers never seem to get it together, you're one of the many amongst us whose good intentions sometimes get swamped by having too many other priorities clamouring for our attention. A friend of mine calls this phenomenon 'life overload'.

To make something happen in our lives, we need to have two particular things going for us – focus and energy. By focus, I'm talking about the ability to apply concentrated attention to a particular task. Energy is about our readiness to take action in pursuit of a chosen outcome. You need to have both in place to be able to pursue a goal in a purposeful manner.

If you are ready to tackle a challenging problem, perhaps the best thing to do is to go back to IDEA 1, *I've got a bit of a problem*. It's Groundhog Day all over again!

Try
another
idea...

Here's my advice. When it comes to making changes in your life, don't succumb to a rather insidious twenty-first-century condition called action-listitis. You know the sort of thing. For example, it's the start of a new year and so you resolve to get fit, lose weight, be nicer to people, learn the bassoon, take up macramé, sort out your finances, mend your bike, redecorate a bedroom or two, write a novel, give up booze, get more sleep, go to the movies more often, get to grips with Sudoku, etc., etc., etc.

'Better to light a candle than to curse the darkness.'
Chinese proverb

Defining
idea...

Drawing up a list with twenty-three action points on it is almost certainly doomed to end in failure. If we manage to achieve four things from the list, the other nineteen stare back off the page at us in silent disappointment.

So rather than create a huge shopping list to take to the self-improvement superstore, pick just one thing to do. Pick the one change you would most like to make and then really apply some focus and energy to making sure it happens.

'Do not be too timid and squeamish about your actions. All life is an experiment.'
RALPH WALDO EMERSON

Defining
idea...

How do you pick that one thing? You need to decide what the most important criteria are for making the choice. For example, it could be the thing that inspires you the most, or it might be something that currently makes you really angry about yourself.

Whatever your choice, remember the words of Doctor Seuss: today is your day! Your mountain is waiting, so...get on your way.

How did it go?

Q OK, I've been thinking about how to take some positive actions based on what I've read. Is there a best place to begin?

A It's true that there are any number of suggestions and ideas that you could choose to take forward from this point. There's no one best way forward, so my suggestion is that you pick out the ones that most appeal or best suit your situation and personality. Then do something with them.

Q I've had a go at implementing a couple of things but I'm finding myself swamped with other commitments. Any suggestions?

A Yes, don't set yourself up to fail. Don't fall into the trap of setting yourself a dozen different things to follow up by the end of next week. You're already a busy person – the chances are that nothing will happen if you set yourself an overwhelming shopping list of things to follow. Far better to identify one action and make sure you follow it through.

Maintain your brain

Here are some tips for keeping your thinking gear in fine fettle.

What I'm about to say shouldn't come as any kind of surprise: your brain is a lifelong work-in-progress.

There's so much we all can do to develop our potential. Take it from me: given the amount of change we can expect to face over the coming decades, lifelong learning is not a trendy concept dreamt up by the human resources department, it's a survival necessity.

So, with an eye to the future, there are a few attributes you might want to consider working on if you're planning to go for more brain upgrades in the years to come. Here are a few suggestions:

COMMIT TO LIFELONG LEARNING

Recognise that the skills, knowledge and experience that got you where you are today won't be enough to get you where you want to be in the future.

'Learning' does not always have to equal 'courses'. Read a book; talk to an expert; surf the net for information; just practice; take a secondment to another part of the business; go and do some work in the community.

Here's an idea for you...

Open yourself to new experiences and insights by experimenting relentlessly (but legally, of course). Become a creature of un-habit: go to a Peter Gabriel concert; take a different route into work; try a different option off the menu; look for one thing, find something else; start a journal or an audio diary; buy a magazine you've never read before; check out a Girls Aloud gig (oops, probably went a bridge too far there).

BECOME A FLUENT COMMUNICATOR: VERBALLY AND IN WRITING

Feel confident that you can give a prepared talk that has style, substance and clarity.

Aim to be 'media-friendly' at all times. It's now pretty much impossible for a politician to succeed without being a skilled communicator. People who are capable at their work but who don't come across well on TV or in person will struggle to move into senior roles in the future.

To polish your writing skills, try reading *The Pyramid Principle* by Barbara Minto, to my mind the best book around on how to present complex ideas in writing.

Work and re-work your CV – it's your career calling card.

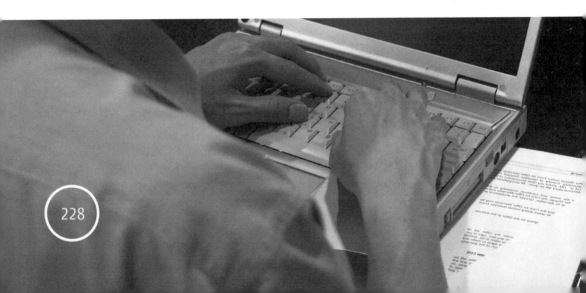

EMBRACE TECHNOLOGY

Fewer than half of Britain's senior directors can send and receive their own emails and 60 per cent are unable to log on to their company's website without help. There may be something faintly comical and endearing about the greybeards struggling to find the on/off switch. However, if you're a thirty- or forty-something with a disdain for new technology, be warned. You can run, but you can't hide.

This idea connects to just about every other idea in the book, so why not close your eyes and open the book at random!

Try another idea...

BE OPPORTUNISTIC

When you're given the chance to try something new, make 'Why not' your default response.

Be spontaneous.

DON'T THINK YOURSELF TO A STANDSTILL

Upgrading your brain involves a mixture of thinking and action. You need both – thinking without action is sterile, action without thinking lacks direction and mindfulness.

As Richard Pascale once put it, it's easier to act yourself into a new way of thinking than to think yourself into a new way of acting.

'Stay hungry, stay foolish.'
STEVE JOBS, CEO of Apple and Pixar

Defining idea...

Defining idea...

'I am always doing things I can't do. That's how I get to do them.'
PABLO PICASSO

You've made a good start in picking up this book (and an even better start if you've read this far!), but in itself it means little. To tweak a cliché: today is your first day with your upgraded brain. So what are you going to do about it?

STAY CURIOUS

For a few nights back in June 2005, the moon appeared to be larger than normal in the night sky. Generally acknowledged at the world's largest optical illusion, even NASA couldn't explain the phenomenon. There's so much we don't know, so much we have yet to experience. Life can be just as entrancing whether you are eight or eighty.

Develop your goals, pursue your dreams, go out and grab your life.

Compose the life you want but don't ignore opportunities to be spontaneous.

Of course, this is nothing like a comprehensive tip-sheet. After all, your brain is a lifelong work-in-progress. So now go off and develop six more ideas of your very own!

Q So is the message here basically 'use it or lose it'?

A To all intents, that's correct. But it's a bit more than that. Actually, we can't help using our brains. Whether we like or not, our brains are at it 24/7 keeping us alive. The whole concept of upgrading our brains is based on the recognition that there is so much more that our brains are capable of. We can extract a much better performance, but it requires commitment, practice and, most of all, a readiness to learn (and sometimes unlearn)

Q What sort of things can we do to improve our mental conditioning?

A As we have seen, there are at least fifty-two possible steps that any of us could take: everything from the highly conceptual to the very practical. The key is to do something. We can all improve our minds, but it does take a bit of effort and focus to achieve this.

How did it go?

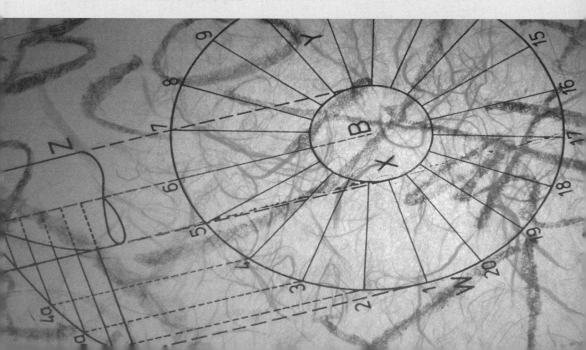

The end...

Or is it a new beginning? We hope that the ideas in this book will have inspired you to try some new things to boost your cognitive powers. Perhaps you've already started reading your newspaper more critically, learned to argue like an ancient Greek or cleared out your physical clutter to give your brain some room to manoeuvre. The insights in this book should have helped you get ahead of the game in both your business and social life.

So why not let us know all about it? Tell us how you got on. What did it for you – what really helped you sharpen your Wildean wit? Maybe you've got some tips of your own you want to share (see next page if so). And if you liked this book you may find we have even more brilliant ideas that could change other areas of your life for the better.

You'll find the Infinite Ideas crew waiting for you online at www.infideas.com.

Or if you prefer to write, then send your letters to:
Upgrade your brain
The Infinite Ideas Company Ltd
36 St Giles, Oxford OX1 3LD, United Kingdom

We want to know what you think, because we're all working on making our lives better too. Give us your feedback and you could win a copy of another *52 Brilliant Ideas* book of your choice. Or maybe get a crack at writing your own.

Good luck. Be brilliant.

Offer one

CASH IN YOUR IDEAS

We hope you enjoy this book. We hope it inspires, amuses, educates and entertains you. But we don't assume that you're a novice, or that this is the first book that you've bought on the subject. You've got ideas of your own. Maybe our author has missed an idea that you use successfully. If so, why not send it to yourauthormissedatrick@infideas.com, and if we like it we'll post it on our bulletin board. Better still, if your idea makes it into print we'll send you four books of your choice or the cash equivalent. You'll be fully credited so that everyone knows you've had another Brilliant Idea.

Offer two

HOW COULD YOU REFUSE?

Amazing discounts on bulk quantities of Infinite Ideas books are available to corporations, professional associations and other organisations.

For details call us on:
+44 (0)1865 514888
Fax: +44 (0)1865 514777
or e-mail: info@infideas.com

Where it's at...

Upgrade your brain: 52 brilliant ideas for everyday genius is part of the acclaimed **52 Brilliant Ideas** series. If you found this book helpful, you may want to take advantage of this special offer exclusive to all readers of *Upgrade your brain*. Choose any two books from the selection below and you'll get one of them free of charge*. See overleaf for prices and details on how to place your order.

brilliant ideas

Cultivate a cool career
Guerilla tactics for reaching the top
By Ken Langdon

Unleash your creativity
52 brilliant ideas for creative genius
By Rob Bevan and Tim Wright

High-impact CVs
Make your résumé sensational
By John Middleton

Enjoy retirement
52 brilliant ideas for loving life after work
By Janet Butwell

Downshift to the good life
Scale it down and live it up
By Lynn Huggins-Cooper

Inspired creative writing
Secrets of the master wordsmiths
By Alexander Gordon Smith

Knockout interview answers
52 brilliant ideas to make job hunting a piece of cake
By Ken Langdon and Nikki Cartwright

Win at the gym
Secrets of fitness and health success
By Steve Shipside

Secrets of wine
Insider insights into the real world of wine
By Giles Kime

Transform your life
2ND EDITION
52 brilliant ideas for becoming the person you want to be
By Penny Ferguson

For more detailed information on these books and others published by Infinite Ideas please visit www.infideas.com

* Postage at £2.75 per delivery address is additional.

Choose any two titles from below and receive the cheapest one free.

Qty	Title	RRP
	Cultivate a cool career	£12.99
	Unleash your creativity	£12.99
	High impact CVs	£12.99
	Enjoy retirement	£12.99
	Downshift to the good life	£12.99
	Inspired creative writing	£12.99
	Knockout interview answers	£12.99
	Win at the gym	£12.99
	Secrets of wine	£12.99
	Transform your life	£12.99
Subtract lowest priced book if ordering two titles		
Add £2.75 postage per delivery address		
Final TOTAL		

Name: ....

Delivery address: ....

....

....

....

E-mail:...Tel (in case of problems): ....

By post Fill in all relevant details, cut out or photocopy this page and send along with a cheque made payable to Infinite Ideas. Send to: *Upgrade your brain* Offer, Infinite Ideas, 36 St Giles, Oxford OX1 3LD, UK.

Credit card orders over the telephone Call +44 (0) 1865 514 888. Lines are open 9am to 5pm Monday to Friday. Just mention the promotion code 'UYBAD07.'

Please note that no payment will be processed until your order has been dispatched. Goods are dispatched through Royal Mail within 14 working days, when in stock. We never forward personal details on to third parties or bombard you with junk mail. This offer is valid for UK and RoI residents only. Any questions or comments please contact us on 01865 514 888 or email info@infideas.com. This offer expires on 31 December 2007.